MW00451343

GEORGE MORTIMER WEST,

HIS PATH IN HISTORY

Compiled from George's diaries by Nancy Hudson

Nancy Hudson
for George

Copyright 2020 by Nancy Hudson

George Mortimer West, His Path in History
Published by Yawn's Publishing
2555 Marietta Hwy, Ste 103
Canton, GA 30114
www.yawnspublishing.com

All rights reserved. No part of this book may be reproduced or transmitted in any form, electronic or mechanical, including photocopying, recording, or data storage systems without the express written permission of the publisher, except for brief quotations in reviews and articles.

The information in this book has been taken from various sources and is presented with no guarantee of its accuracy. All photographs used were submitted for this publication. We assume no liability for the accuracy of the information presented or any photos used without permission.

Library of Congress Control Number: 2020905757

ISBN13: 978-1-947773-71-4

Printed in the United States

Cover photo is the front door of the William West home, Scituate, RI, taken around 1918.

Author photo on back cover by Andrew Wardlow Photography

Contents

To All:

Whom I trust will study the past, as well as look to the future, and always remember that "People who take no pride in the noble achievements of remote ancestors will never achieve anything worthy to be remembered with pride by remote ancestors."
George M. West, 1919. (Quoting Thomas B. Macaulay)

Photo by George M. West

PREFACE

In 2019 the Panama City Publishing Company Museum was provided access to stored boxes of West family documents, letters, deeds, and photos. For those interested in the museum, the West family, the history of Panama City, George M. West, and Lillian Carlisle West, the boxes were like sifting through a treasure chest. Each document was inspected, many donated to the museum and preserved. Initially, temporary displays for the museum were developed from the material. Then, it became apparent there was so much information to share that it should be written and preserved for the future. After all, George West is credited as a Founding Father of Panama City, and what would it be had he not come here? In the process of sifting through hundreds of documents, letters, and diaries George came to life and we are able to know him. He wrote "...*we will close this record and lay it away to someday be brought forward and studied over with more pain or pleasure than its perusal gives me now.*" Indeed his life was quite painful. Interwoven throughout you will find diary entries, poems, letters, art, photographs, news paper excerpts, and stories of his ambitious enterprises and events in his life, and the people around him. This documentation is directly from the diaries and papers of George West. It is his story, in his words. Some dates, years, names, spellings and other information may be inconsistent or incorrect for unknown reasons, but is presented directly from the writings of George West. Much more can be learned from the Panama City Pilot and St. Andrews Bay Newspapers available online at www.flhiddentreasures-.com and from the St. Andrews Buoy online at https://ufdc.ufl.edu/. George's own spellings of words are used except on some occasions for better identification. He would write "bought supplies & c." the "c" meaning "such". He used initials or a first name only to identify people and when known, the full name has been added.

Many thanks to Charles "Buddy" West for saving this history and sharing George and Lillian West with us all. Thank you to Margaret West Matheson for your unfailing support. Also a special thank you to the Local History Room at the Bay County Public Library for preserving precious diaries and photographs, and the expert assistance. Particularly Laura Moree, Lorrie Canfijn and Abbie Beck. Photographs from there are noted as "BCPL".

NEW YORK TO WISCONSIN

Imagine Oneida County, New York, December 24th, 1814 when Philander Bailey West was the 6th generation of Wests born in America. Oneida County is not far from Lake Ontario and though the craft of making silverware was its primary business, as a young man Philander worked at farming and teaching school. He married Fidelia Mason on April 15th, 1841. Their first son, Charles Arthur West was born just a year later on April 12th, 1842. Their second son, George Mortimer West was born November 28th, 1845. The first twins known in the family, Ellen M. and Helen M. West, were born to Philander and Fidelia on November 17th, 1849. The trait for twins may have been introduced into the West family through Fidelia, as there would be other twins in this lineage of the West family from this point. In these lines from a letter to George in 1904, his maternal Aunt Maria describes young George:

"Today many events in your entire life, up to the present time, have passed through my mind. You are my oldest nephew living and I remember you from babyhood. The first time I took you in my arms you were a squirming, wrestling pink and white baby, and soon grew into a bright active restless little boy that didn't want Aunt Maria to come to their house because she would bathe him when she came, then when old enough to go to school, and learn lessons, soon tired of it for the reason that the teacher couldn't hear him write his lessons as soon as he learned them."

Philander Bailey West, P. B. as he was known by friends and family, went to Wisconsin in 1856 and secured a job as an agent with the Milwaukee Horicon & Ohio Railway Company (M. H. & O.) in Brandon. The town and railroad were new and was founded on the manufacturing of hemp rope. Fidelia and the children joined him there in 1857.

P.B. and Fidelia experienced much heartbreak in their lives, and he left behind a collection of poems authored by him that provide a glimpse of his talent. In 1919 George collected his father's poems and placed those into an envelope. There are poems about death, often published in newspapers alongside obituaries. But there are also poems devoted to the wind, the stars, and flowers. One could speculate that P. B.'s son, George, derived his interest in horticulture from his father, as well as an interest in writing and weather. George did follow in his father's steps as a railroad employee.

Shortly after the family joined P. B. in Brandon, young Charles went to work for the M. H. & O. Railway Company, then its successor, the Milwaukee and St. Paul Company. His last position there was as a Freight Train Conductor.

Tragedy struck the family when Helen died of diphtheria in 1859 at the age of 9. The West family was again devastated at home when 20-year-old Charles died of diphtheria in December of 1862. Just 5 days later, the deadly virus took the life of 13-year-old Ellen. George also contracted diphtheria during this time. He survived and became the sole living child of P. B. and Fidelia. The 1904 letter from Aunt Maria gives a glimpse of that time: "...*your own fearful sickness followed, for weeks you hovered upon the brink of the river and you well-nigh entered 'The valley of the shadow,' but you were spared that your parents might not be totally bereaved and have no one to care nor provide for them in their declining years.*"

According to George, the girls and Charles were buried in Union Prairie Cemetery, Brandon, Wisconsin. George had the West family marker erected in 1888 for a cost of $235. However, the family members are actually buried in Brandon Cemetery. The Brandon Times states Fidelia West was buried at Union Prairie in 1875, but in fact, the location is Brandon Cemetery. It is unclear as to why George wrote in his diary and the Brandon Times published that the burials are in Union Prairie, unless the cemetery names were changed at some point.

West Marker at Brandon Cemetery, GMW Collection, BCPL

West Family marker and 5 markers with plants on top of graves of (L to R) Philander B. and Fidelia   (GMW's parents), Helen, Ellen, and Charles Aurthur (GMW's siblings), GMW Collection, BCPL

Today, below and to the right of the West marker are (L to R): Charles Ernest (GMW's son), Eleanor "Nellie" West (Charles' wife), Ernest (infant twin to Philip, GMW's grandsons), and Adella (GMW's first wife). The 5 markers in the top left are those pictured above with plants growing on the graves. Courtesy Brandon Historical Society.

In January, 1891, George began writing his family history. He wrote this about himself:

...Born in Sangerfield, Oneida County, N. Y., November 28, 1845. Removed to Wisconsin with the family in 1857, and in 1860-61 learned telegraphy at Waupun, Wis., while assisting at station work on the Milwaukee & Horicon Railway. Remained in the employ of that company and its successor the Milwaukee & St. Paul, as helper, operator, and agent until 1870; having been appointed agent at Brandon, Wis., by S. S. Merrill, in the fall of 1863. He established the Brandon Times February 17th, 1866, and continued its publication until the fall of 1871, when he sold the same, and with E. H. Merrell, of Ripon College, bought the Ripon Free Press. Its publication was carried on by

them until the spring of 1873, when they sold the paper. He was admitted to the Bar in the municipal court at Ripon, Wis., May 6th, 1873. Removed to the Upper Peninsula of Michigan in June, 1873, and entered the employ of the Chicago & North-Western Railway on the 17th of that month, as operator and car dispatcher, at New York Mine, near Ishpeming. Removed to Escanaba, Michigan, August 8th, 1873, and was thereupon appointed Train Dispatcher of the Peninsula Division. Was appointed Assistant Superintendent in November, 1886. He was united in marriage to Adella Melvina Showers, July 16th, 1865, at her residence in Lamartine, Fond Du Lac County, Wisconsin. They have had born to them one son, Charles Ernest, and one daughter who died soon after birth, and was buried at Escanaba."

Rail yard, Brandon, Wisconsin, GMW Collection

George Mortimer West as a young man, GMW Collection, BCPL

As was common for the time, George began working at age 15, in 1860, in Brandon and Waupun which was about 8 miles away. In 1866 at just 21 years old he established the Brandon Times newspaper, a weekly in Brandon, Wisconsin. The office of the paper was located at the depot in Brandon at this time. George frequently printed his father's poetry in the paper. He sold the Brandon Times in October of 1871.

From the Diaries

1873

In May of 1873 George was finalizing his studies to become an attorney and was admitted to the bar shortly thereafter. Charles was only 5 at this time and became ill with diphtheria. Adella was constantly battling various illnesses and ailments, and she was also ill at the same time. George was only 27 years old at this time, and after having lost his brother and sisters to diphtheria he must have been very fearful at this point. In a few days Charles recovered, as did Adella.

One month later George embarked on a train trip north to Michigan's Upper Peninsula, along with others, exploring opportunities with the Milwaukee, Horicon, and Ohio Railroad. He visited the New York Mine near Ishpeming, Michigan. On this trip George was plagued with an illness, and commented in his diary about taking a vinegar bath, bathing in the creek at night, and the days being dull. He did a lot of reading, took long walks, slept little, wrote to Dell (as he called Adella) often, and felt "blue".

As a result of the trip George moved to Ishpeming, Michigan in June, 1873 and began working for the Chicago & North Western Railway Company (C. & N. W.) Dell and Charles remained almost 200 miles away in Brandon but frequently traveled by train or wagon to visit George. He was a witness to history nearby in the Upper Peninsula when Michigamme Township burned and he wrote in his diary on June 19th, 1873:

"a terrible windy day – Michigamme burned down this forenoon – several lives lost"

A passing Marquette, Houghton, and Ontonagon passenger train drove through the flames to pick up as many people as possible. Over 100 homes were destroyed by the forest fire, but the saw mill was spared. Within the week, the mill was up and running; and over the next 6 months 300 houses and other buildings were constructed and the township recovered.

George moved to Escanaba, Michigan by August that year taking the position of Train Dispatcher, which he held until 1886. He found a house at 321 Harrison (Adella's diary says 329 Harrison) just a few blocks walk from his office.

George's father was employed by the railroad and other work in Brandon until 1874. P. B. and Fidelia moved to Escanaba, Michigan and resided there with George and Dell. Fidelia was in poor health and succumbed to asthma at the age of 59 on May 14th, 1875. P. B. continued to live with George and Dell until his death.

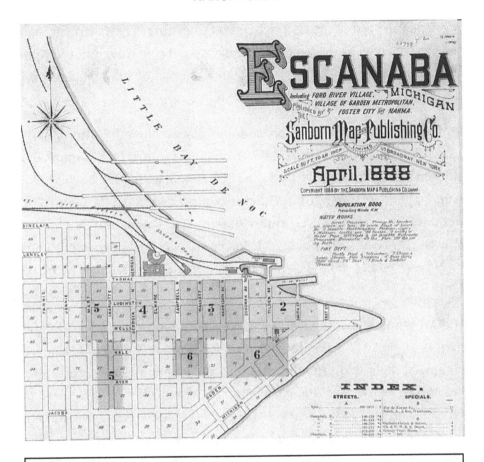

Map of a portion of Escanaba showing the rail yard, ore docks, and Harrison Avenue south of the yard. GMW Collection.

George was attentive to keeping a diary and that collection provides a glimpse of daily life and his interests. Most of his entries are about work he did each day, purchases he made, cash in and cash out for various work, loans, and equipment, the weather, and the health of family members. At work he managed the time table for the train operations, scheduling men and trains, travelling the rail line by train to check his times, from 90–200 miles in a day. In his diary he noted the number of train cars of freight, including lumber, syrup, cattle, and ore. The rail yard easily had over 4,000 train cars dispatched through the yard each week during the warm seasons. From November to April the business would slack off due to the closure of the adjacent port during the winter icing over of the lake.

Purchases he made and recorded in his diary included: Buttons (.10), candy (.10 to .20), and medicine (.75). Sleeve buttons (1.25), meat and chicken (.50 to .75 for both), oil can (.50), candle wick (.05), butter (.65), laundry (.55), lettuce (.10), 100 pictures printed for 5.00, Vaseline (.20), Borax (.05), a shave (.15), shoes (8.00), and a new hat (2.50). The Wests' Christmas shopping list for friends and family sometimes included a book (.25), hairpins (.70), perfume (1.00), and a match box (.10).

Life was not all work. George wrote about attending socials and dances, boat rides, going for sleigh rides, snow shoe walks, "taking ice cream" at night with friends, attending the lodge, masquerades at the music hall, ice skating, and gardening. He went to the theatre when in Chicago and enjoyed opera and plays such as *My Geraldine* and *Palma*. In winter he watched his son Charles play ice polo. In summer when the lake thawed he enjoyed the yacht races. He built a conservatory on to his house and grew roses, carnations, geraniums, crocus, tulips, hyacinth, plumbago, begonias, asters, daisies, marigolds, primroses, Lilly of the valley, pansies, coleus, chrysanthemums, gladiolus, sunflowers, bachelor buttons, orchids, and many more varieties. He hired men to perform other maintenance and chores around his property, but the gardening was reserved for him. He would hoe the weeds, made planting trenches, and put in his seeds including sweet peas, radishes, beets, yellow beans, onions, strawberries, nicotine, and cucumbers. He built the trellises for the vines and kept the garden weeded. Gardening was a passion for him and he found it productive, peaceful, and rejuvenating. He was intrigued by the beauty of the flowers and often attempted to grow a variety of new plants. George, Dell, and Charlie took walks in the nearby hills to pick raspberries.

West home showing conservatory addition, and Dell, at 321 Harrison, Escanaba, Michigan, c. 1885, GMW Collection, BCPL and Margaret West Matheson

He papered the ceilings and his father painted the walls in the house, and George put storm windows up each year in the fall, and took them down in April. He took up art and painted miniatures of flowers in his diary. Reading was also a favorite pastime for George and his interests were vast. A sampling of his reading list can be found in the appendix.

1879

There are no known diaries for 1874-1878, but in 1879 George began a new diary and wrote about the weather, the production of lumber (mostly cedar) at the mill, the number of train car loads of lumber and ore, engines getting off track (a common issue in the winter when the tracks froze and would break), hiring men to build a well, getting hay in for the cattle, and writing new time tables for the trains. Trains were frequently in trouble from snow drifts sometimes over 18' high. From May 1st through November 1st ships brought cargo into the port adjacent to the rail yard then were loaded with ore and departed for other locations. Some of the ships were: *Lady Washington, Steam Barge Massachusetts, Daisy Moore*, the sailing vessel *Richards, Kingfisher, Fairbanks*, the *Swain* tug, *Sea Swallow*, the *Anderson* tug, *Manhattan, H.A. Tuttle, Panther*, and *Aurora*.

In early spring George agreed to deliver a lecture on the "Antiquity of Man & Evolution". He wrote the lecture and developed a chart he would present. March 18th he wrote about the monetary value of his research and writing for the lecture *"Tis taken up 6 days – $83.72 worth."*

Many times throughout the diaries George commented that he felt blue, gloomy, lifeless, spiritless, dull, and that the winter weather was relentless and bitter.

May 23rd …will it never warm up – it is so cold it fairly chills the marrow in ones bones – and makes one feel that it would be more comfortable in the grave

Quite possibly the daughter George refers to in his biography was born to Dell on May 29th this year. The infant died at birth and was buried in Escanaba.

Throughout the diaries depression and sad days follow one after the other, then George periodically had better days. He never expressed feeling joy or happiness, but only feeling "better" or "good". Working for a railroad company was difficult and arduous work. The conditions of long hours, harsh weather, and physical danger were stressful. For all the hard work there was little recognition or appreciation from the company. Personal satisfaction of a job well done and the pay car arriving on time were the rewards. George was extremely punctual and making sure the trains ran on time was important both for him personally and for safety. He had to manage keeping trains from ending up on the same track at the same time and colliding. The time card he wrote up and distributed to the Engineers had to be strictly followed by them to avoid disaster. He was often writing a new card based on the fluctuation of business in cargo and passenger service.

During the time George lived there were many challenges not commonly experienced today. Illness, primitive medical and dental care, none of the modern conveniences at home or work that subsequent generations have enjoyed, all made life difficult and many times too short. George suffered frequently from toothaches, winter colds, and rheumatism in his back and legs. It was common for railroad workers to be injured, maimed, and even killed on the job. Running water inside the house was a luxury. But people in this time period found a way to do the necessary things each day and still have plenty of time for socializing and being with friends and family. In August George, Dell, and several friends decided to take a vacation and go on a camping trip. They boarded the No. 8 train and travelled about 49 miles west to Quinnesec, Michigan where they got off the train at 2:00 PM and hiked 2 miles to the Upper Falls, on the Menominee River. They arrived at a good camping site at 5:00. The next 3 days were spent fishing for bass, canoeing, and hiking to other falls.

He closed each year in his diary with a summary and hope for the future. In this closing entry, he actually pondered that his diaries would be read one day in the future.

December 31st As the year commenced with a snow – so does it close – This AM we have a snow storm – The storm is over old mother Earth wrapped in a winding sheet of dazzling whiteness and only awaits the hour of 12 – to take into her arms the young new year – and change her windy sheet into a christening robe – The most eventful year of my life is near its close – Can another ever furnish such labor – trouble – torment as this – I trust not – and trusting this we will close this record and lay it away to someday be brought forward and studied over with more pain or pleasure than its perusal gives me now – It is idle to speculate on the future – the past is strange enough – nothing that can come will exceed its strangeness that which is past – But may the future be more pleasant than has been the honored year of 1879 – Farewell

1880

On first day of 1880, we find the first glimpse of George dreaming of the south:

January 1st Clear skies usher in the New Year – and the winding sheet of 1879 now seems as a regal christening robe for 1880 – the land of orange blossoms and perpetual summer sends through natures messenger the mild south wind – greeting to the northern pines and cedars – a dull cheerless day to me....

January 7th Cloudy, mild ....Called at printing office in PM and set up half a stick of type – the first in many years.

Dell was "sick abed" most of February and George pressed forward with his work on the railroad through to the spring. He dealt with train wrecks, a strike by railroad employees, and the fierce winter weather. Finally by the middle of May he was able to work in his garden which always improved his state of mind. During the summer months he built a barn and had construction of the conservatory started on his house. At work he managed the largest week's work ever on the Peninsula Division, hauling 6,836 loaded cars through the railroad yard and 6,570 empties. In mid-October the *"worst storm ever known in this country"* hit the area and blew down the barn George had built in the summer.

December 31ˢᵗ – This ends 1880 – WBL (William B. Linsley, GMW's supervisor at work) *returned today from Cleveland – a dull – quiet day to me – as so many others have been in the year past – Will 1881 bring no more joyous days – spend the coming at that office – The year finds me as it began – but older than the calendar would show.*

1881

This year began as many others for George. Dell was ill frequently. Her side, back, and head had "hard pain". After several days of snow, below zero temperatures, and snow drifts of 18-23 feet, George was on Engine 305 trying to clear track and find crews from abandoned trains. After work, he did have his conservatory where he was able to spend time starting plants, cutting blooms, and making bouquets for friends and family.

May 16ᵗʰ This book has been sadly neglected but today I will try to recall the past month and note down the prominent incidents – if there are any – All days are alike to me

May 30ᵗʰ Still raining...Set out good many plants – Sent for plants to Milwaukee –Made coleus bed – Have 50 geraniums in one bed – getting office work in better shape.

June 25ᵗʰ...Saw Comet tonight for the first time in the Northwest – very bright with fan shape tail about 10 or 12 (degrees) in length

The comet he witnessed was the Great Comet of 1881, a long-period comet discovered by John Tebbutt on May 22, 1881 at Windsor, New South Wales. It was called a "great comet" because of its brightness at its last apparition. George observed the comet again over the next few nights.

Great Comet of 1881 photographed by Henry Draper using a mirror to create a wide-angle and capture the entire tail in one photograph. This was the first photograph of a comet.

The next couple of months George and all American citizens followed any news they could find about the assassination of President Garfield. George recorded in his diary:

July 2nd Clear – warm day – Rcvd the news at 9:30 this am of attempted assassination of Pres Garfield by Guiteau....

President Garfield was shot by Charles Julius Guiteau at the Baltimore and Potomac Railroad Station. Many people, and possibly George, were suspicious that former Collector of the Port of New York, Roscoe Conkling, and former Collector, now Vice President Chester Arthur, had a hand in the assassination. The position of Collector of the Port of New York was the highest paid Federal job in the United States. When Conkling left the position he had made sure Arthur succeeded him as a reward for Arthur's allegiance to the Stalwarts, also known as "Conklingites". The Stalwarts of the Republican Party were mostly from former Confederate states, and existed in the 1870's – 1880's. They were against the Pendleton Civil Service Reform Act, which would require Federal positions be filled based on merit, not political patronage. The rest of the Republican Party was in favor of the Reform Act. However after Garfield's death on September 20th Arthur ascended to President and did sign the Reform Act.

George continued work, gardening, and making bouquets. He took up painting and pasted miniature paintings he made into his diary. On September 14th he recorded an aurora of unique shape in the night sky:

"... A very curious display of aurora tonight – a broad lens shaped white light directly overhead extending from SE to NW at 8PM very bright."

October 17th painted abutilon

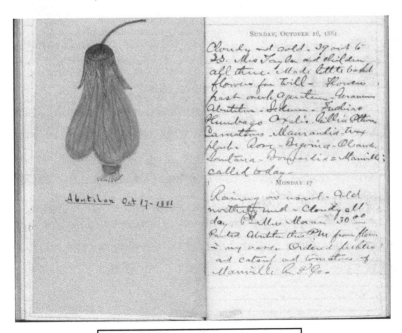

George West Diaries, BCPL

Charles was 15 years old and he went hunting with his father in the fall. George must have been pleased as he wrote that Charles had shot his first game, a partridge and a rabbit. The railroad work continued to be grueling as George wrote that he and his colleague were *"convinced that there are other occupations more valuable than railroading"*.

December 31ˢᵗ Cloudy – cold northwest wind – A few scattering flakes of snow drifting in the air afraid to light on the cold bare earth – The last day of 1880 was to me blue enough – but this day finds me more despondent than ever before – 1881 has given me some pleasure – but the bottom of the cup has been wormwood and gall – and I have drained it to the dregs – I find myself in a physical condition far from pleasant to contemplate – will '82 better anything – to me now there is ......but pleasant thoughts of the future – Mr. Thompson's folks visit at our home this evening – very quiet day.

George was a member of the Methodist Episcopal Church in Escanaba. He wrote often about stopping by to visit "Mr. T". The "Mr. and Mrs. T" George referred to frequently were Rev. Henry and Millie Thompson. George often stopped to visit them in the evenings and enjoyed conversations, but also George took the collection to Rev. Thompson. In those times a collection was often taken up by an appointed member going around to the houses of each congregation member and whatever was given was taken directly to the pastor. It was common for members to donate anything including money, chickens, fabric, eggs, flour, meat, oil, or whatever goods they had to share with their pastor. For a time George delivered this collection to the Thompsons.

1882

Early in this year George was able to get away for a couple of days by train to Brandon. He visited old acquaintances and all around town including the cemetery and Union Prairie School where he had attended 23 years prior. In 1885 when he acquired a camera he went back again and photographed the cemetery, school, and other places. After this trip he wrote *"Rain – Snow – clouds and sunshine all in 12 hours. A fair explanation of my feelings"* and how he was tired of this life and wished he could dispose of everything and go somewhere else.

Union Prairie School,
Brandon, Wisconsin,
GMW Collection, BCPL

George awoke at 5:30 one January morning so cold he could not sleep any longer, so he got up and painted the little Fuchsia branch for practice. The house inset on the Fuchsia stem is unknown.

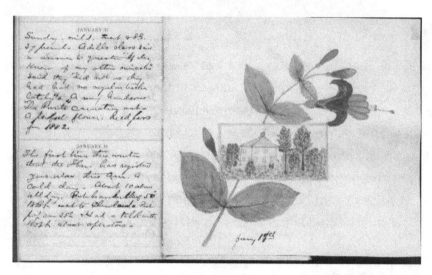

George West Diaries, BCPL

Dell was ill again and George pondered his life:

"A dull day. Not enough to do to keep me from feeling gloomy. What is this change I feel & why? Does Time conquer all? Or is Human Nature like a pendulum – forever swinging from one extreme to the other?"

The railroad announced that George had been serving as Apprentice Assistant Superintendent, but it was the first he had heard of this. He committed to himself to try and dispose of outside property and start saving cash for an unknown venture in the future. Life had always been payday to payday for him. In spite of the shortage of funds and Dell's illness, they managed to host the Methodist Episcopal Sociable at their home in late February, with 45 attending.

Each April the port adjacent to the rail yard reopened and as the ice melted on the bay the first ships began to come in to port with their cargo to unload. Once reloaded, they set sail to deliver the goods from

Escanaba. The melting ice shifted in springtime squalls and sheets of it could pile up as much as 20 feet high by 800 long and 50 to 100 feet wide on the shore. The sound of the ice being shoved around could be loud at times. It was sometimes June before all the ice was gone, though in May there could be as many as 45 ships surrounded by broken ice already in the harbor.

Ice in the harbor at Escanaba, GMW Collection, BCPL

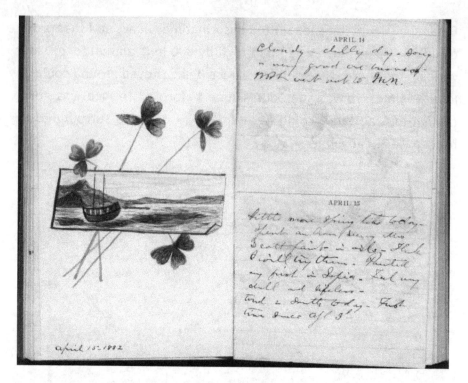

George West Diaries, BCPL

September 25th George must have been pleased to write *"Charlie commenced work in office today – his first position"*. Charles took his first job on the railroad at age 16. From George's genealogy papers about the career of his son Charles:

"...Commenced work as a messenger in the general office of the Chicago & North-Western Ry, at Escanaba, September 25, 1882, where he learned telegraphy. Was appointed operator at South Y office in Escanaba in the Fall of 1883; promoted to Dispatcher's operator in the Dispatcher's office, Escanaba, August 18, 1884, and to Train Dispatcher December 10, 1886."

In November and December heavenly displays continued to capture George's attention with what he called *"A very extensive electric show commenced early this am - At 5:30 the whole heavens was consumed with a flame colored Aurora"*. Then on a trip to Chicago for railroad work he was able to see Venus through a telescope at the Grand Pacific Hotel.

1883

The first mention of Florida comes in February 1883 when he called on Major Newcombe and they talked of Florida. There are no details of the conversation. In the spring George's roses and hyacinths were out in profusion, but George was feeling dull. He wrote of having no ambition, no life, and wishing he could feel different. As the weather warmed he felt better, went fishing for trout, and joined friends on picnics to Squaw Point, about 6 miles NE across the Little Bay De Noch, the north end of Lake Michigan.

They travelled in small sailboats and launches to the point and spent the afternoon. The summer abruptly ended in September with a hard freeze and killed his garden plants. As winter set in he again became *"So blue I do nothing but commune with my thoughts — which are gloomy enough."*

Dec 31st 16 degrees above — a little snow falling this am. Wind north ......started for Chicago this PM — Dell — Ella — Minnie and myself...at 10 PM go to bed in sleeper. Thus passes the old year — a year of change to me and to the Division — E. H. White and WBL — both gone and our prospects not improved by Mr. L's (Linsley's) successor — Ten years of earnest service for the Company have apparently brought no corresponding reward and under the new regime we start out de novo (from the beginning) - with the rest I am depressed and feel that my

25

tenure of office is no better than the others. Liable at any time to be thrust aside through the strange freaks of one who cannot maintain himself for two years in his present position – as he now runs it. Again I am called to face the future as I was ten years ago – and must prepare for it. My health is about the same as a year ago – except that from tiresome pains in my back when riding or early in the morning – which cautions me to do something for them – financially I have gained a little. During the year I have paid some old debts and today have a hundred and twenty dollars more than a year ago in the bank. I have not been extravagant in my personal account – and that which I have expended has given me much pleasure. If I can keep my present salary for the coming year I ought to be very near free from debt by 1885. I ought to secure something outside of railroading for a rainy day or a change – The year has been one of sunshine and shadow to me personally – clear and pleasant in its morning and forenoon – cloudy and cheerless in its fall and winter- Oh for a day of June once more – what would I not give for it.

1884

Though winters found George gloomy most of the time, he was again attracted to the night sky and the display of yet another comet and other spectacular views of Venus and the stars.

January 15th ...the comet quite bright tonight – a sabre tail and head like a star of the 2nd magnitude...

This comet George viewed was the Comet of 1812 and 1846. In 1884 it was making another pass within view from earth as it again travelled the path, spanning from near the orbit of Mars to beyond the orbit of Neptune.

January 20th A clear cold night. The stars show in great numbers and the SW with the zodiacal light colored by the peculiar red of our twilights nowadays – with Venus in its base – the comet alone – and a range of bright stars extending to its outer limits – presents a sight to be long remembered.

The purchase of a Mullikens Amateur Photo kit was the beginning of George's photography. He noted in his diary when he took photographs and the subject. This record has made it possible to identify many of the photographs in the extensive collection. The kit included a camera, developing supplies and oil burning "lantern" projector. Transparent glass slides with photographs on them could be cast to a wall. Taking photographs opened a whole new world for George, and Charles was at his father's side as they experimented with this new camera together. They took pictures at the rail yard, the docks, and on outings to Squaw Point.

Ore docks at Escanaba, GMW Collection, BCPL

Ore carts in Escanaba Railyard, GMW Collection, BCPL

Railyard at Escanaba, GMW Collection, BCPL

Beached at Squaw Point, GMW Collection, BCPL

In early February George noted another peculiar celestial display and documented it by sketching the phenomenon in his diary.

February 3rd ...a very peculiar white circle at 6:50 this evening – directly overhead – laying horizontal about 40 degrees = diameter - the moon on its southwestern circumference – nearly clear – very little cirrus clouds – only lasted a few minutes.

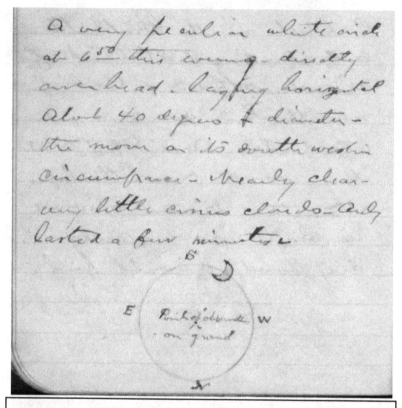

George West Diaries, BCPL

For the July 4th celebration George had the task of setting off the fireworks for the town, and Charles helped him. Shortly after this holiday the circus train arrived and once set up, the Wests and their friends attended. George paid $3.25 total for his family to attend the circus and they all stayed until 11:00PM.

George and Charles cleaned up the small boat they had and took trips across the bay to Lighthouse Point, loaded the boat with friends for the Sunday School picnic at Squaw Point, and enjoyed some time on the water. George and Charles took overnight trips to camp at Squaw Point to hunt and fish.

A Sunday School picnic gathering at Squaw Point, GMW
Collection, BCPL

George's photography skills grew better and he produced enough good glass slides to put on a lantern show for his Sunday School class. A collection was taken and he actually ended up being paid $8.15 for putting on the slide show.

Dec 31ˢᵗ ....thus ends '84, a year that has been very unsatisfactory to me and one that has worn me out more than any two heretofore – There has been but little of June and many months of glooming November – I have learned much about photography in the year – have added to the house – and paid some debts. But take it all in all I have not saved a great deal toward a rainy day from a liberal salary – and the rainy days may come soon – I am not quite as well as a year ago – and ambition fades with the increasing years – I am very despondent tonight – and have seen many such nights in the last year – may '85 prove to be more pleasant.

1885

In January this year George was doing research and putting together another lantern show to present in February. One could take "views" for your own slides, or glass slides could be purchased with a variety of photographs on them. Images of popular buildings and sites around the world could light up the wall in a home. On February 25ᵗʰ George conducted the lantern show for the Grand Army of the Republic and about 600 attended his presentation. The GAR was a fraternal organization composed of veterans who served in the American Civil War in the Union Army, Navy, and Marines. Predominantly in the north, they advocated voting rights for black veterans, patriotic education, and veterans' pensions. The GAR eventually became partisan and supported Republican candidates. The group helped make Memorial Day an annual national holiday. George noted in his diary the presentation was a big success.

He began experimenting with a microscope lens on the camera and took close ups in his conservatory. Dell's health continued to fluctuate with frequent illness. In May she contracted malaria and eventually recovered. They helped with the Children's Day at church, attended school graduation, and had a veranda constructed at the house.

In July George noticed a boat at the docks. The *Jane Anderson* had come in to deliver 28 bushels of oats and George really liked the boat. He wrote to the owner, Mrs. Bellows, and inquired about a deal. He offered her $250.00 for half ownership in the vessel. She accepted his offer and George then located Capt. Hewitt and bargained to pay him $6.00 a day to operate the vessel. August 24th George and his party of friends and family set out for a week trip on the *Jane Anderson*. He took along his camera and diary, and documented the trip in his first book ever published *The Cruise of the Jane Anderson*. Only eleven copies

were printed. They were gifts for each person on the cruise. The scanned book is available through the Bay County Public Library Local History Room.

Original map of the cruise on the *Jane Anderson*, West Documents Collection

Vessels in harbor at
Escanaba, Michigan,
photo taken by George
c. 1880's, GMW
Collection, BCPL

In the fall a railroad strike kept George busy. He also made additional improvements at home by purchasing a furnace to heat the house in the winter. The house had just a fireplace prior to this.

It was customary for the family to go to the woods and find a tree on December 24th each year. They brought one home, set it up on the table, decorated it, then with everyone gathered around they opened gifts on Christmas Eve. Christmas day was then spent calling on friends and family, ice skating, and reading. George always received at least one new book, and usually handkerchiefs, candy, moccasins, and other items.

At the end of the year he created a small booklet with a poem and he painted the first page of the poem.

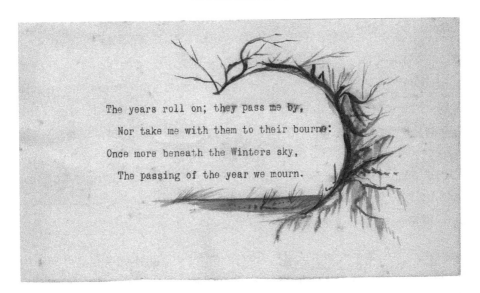

The years roll on; they pass me by,
Nor take me with them to their bourne:
Once more beneath the Winters sky,
The passing of the year we mourn.

West Documents Collection

December 31ˢᵗ 30 degrees, cloudy. Fire at 5 this am in Coach in yard. Pd 25c chemicals. Fixed up the live lantern today – have exhibition this evening for Sunday School. Pleasant time – Dull day. Dell's cold no better – Girls all to rink, polo tonight – wrote a little this am. Poetry. Cloudy but mild all day – Mr & Mrs T stop a few minutes in the evening. So closes 1885, a year of saddened pleasure – From first to last it has been all but cheerless. Occasionally a bright oasis was met with – but the desert surrounded it and we journeyed on – will 1886 prove better? I see no promise of it. I feel that I am growing older - not in my feelings but in the flesh. Life ceases of pleasure in it each succeeding year – and fewer friendships I know I ought to take a rest and vacation but cannot afford it. Have saved some money during the past year – Made many improvements – but the trials – the changes – have worn upon me sadly. May 1886 be brighter – more kind to me.

1886

George received notice from the Chicago & North Western Railroad on January 1ˢᵗ that he was appointed Assistant Superintendent. He was no longer an apprentice. In the evening he and Charles cooked oysters and feasted. He was insecure in his new position and a little unsure. It did come with some pay increase, but also the possibility he would never move any further up in the company. There was competition for positions in management and once in a position they wanted, people would stay until death.

In April George met with Capt. Hewitt and purchased a piece of oak to repair the keel of the *Jane Anderson*. He travelled to Chicago on business and attended the Grand Opera House where he saw the new comic opera *The Mikado* by Gilbert and Sullivan. It had opened in London the previous year and had one of the longest runs of any opera to that time. The Grand Opera House in Chicago was constructed in 1874 and had changed hands more than once since then. It opened as the Grand Opera House in 1880, and in 1902 featured the premier of *The Wizard of Oz*, and in 1903 the premier of *Babes in Toyland*. The Grand Opera House was torn down in 1958.

P. B. West was aging and his heart was failing. George stayed by his father's side.

August 24ᵗʰ 86 degrees, clear. A warm day – I slept some last night in lounge – Father failed all night -really low this AM. At 10:25 I asked him if he would have some water. He nodded and said yes. I gave it to him and letting his head back on pillow he quietly breathed his last at 10:32 am. So passes away the last link that binds me to my childhood – and the last one of his generation – a very warm sultry day. Took up my work in office this PM.

The next day George prepared to accompany his father's remains to Brandon via train. Rev. Thompson went along. They arrived there at 10:20 AM on the next day, then Kelly Funeral Home took over and for the $14.50 George paid, Philander Bailey West was buried at Brandon Cemetery.

In the fall Dell was ill and required a surgical procedure for which she was administered ether for the first time. Upon her quick recovery, George resumed daily life. He and Charles spent time rowing to Portage Island, duck hunting, and Charles typed as George dictated "The Cruise of the Jane Anderson". The 11 copies of his first published book were delivered to George by the end of the year.

December 31st ...So ends 1886. A year of trials and sorrows time – with no great pleasure. Many radical changes have I experienced in various ways – but none bring any great benefit to me – some great losses. I see no prospects for any change that will benefit me. I begin to dread the long winters here and long for a more favored clime. I am adrift as to what to look to in the future – I have less confidence in the friendships of those I would were my friends – and feel that the coming years are to still further separate me from the friends of the past. I care not to speculate on 1887. It can bring on nothing worse than 1886 has furnished.

1887

The New Year found George calling on friends, taking sleigh rides, and spending half a day on the toboggan slide. He and Dell shopped for new furniture and selected a lounge chair, sideboard, and bookcase. On March 6th he decided to make his first trip to Florida, and left the very next day. He sold some lots he owned and had $250.00 cash on hand for the trip. Unfortunately, he must have temporarily misplaced his diary. The entries resume on the train returning from Florida. However, while in St. Andrews he made arrangements to purchase the property that had been the former Gov. John Clark home site on today's Beach Drive. On September 29th the deed was executed and George paid $700 for the 4 lots, existing house, and other structures. He returned to Escanaba after 3 weeks away and had travelled 2,953 miles.

The year went along as usual until he prepared to return to St. Andrews on December 6th. In preparation he ordered peach and other fruit trees to be shipped to St. Andrews. Rev. Henry Thompson was one of the friends to accompany George on this next trip south. The train stopped in Nashville and the group had the morning to take in some sights. Rev. Thompson had fought in the Civil War 23 years earlier and was located at the Rains house during the Battle of Nashville in December 1864. George and Rev. Thompson were able to locate the Rains house and visit the nearby battlefield. Rev. Thompson reminisced and they picked up bullets. Maj. Gen. William T. Sherman had split off on his March to the Sea, leaving Maj. Gen. George H. Thomas to hold Tennessee. Maj. Gen. Thomas's army, including Rev. Thompson, defeated Confederate leader Lt. Gen. John Bell Hood and his army in what was hailed as one of the Union Army's largest victories.

The group arrived in Marianna on December 8th with George having spent a total of $9.68 from Escanaba to Marianna. They tarried in Marianna and with Capt. Phillips toured Blue Spring, Greenwood, and enjoyed a pleasant ride around the Florida country. The next day, they set out for St. Andrews in buggies and covered wagons. The route took them around Compass Pond, and they settled for the night on Juniper Creek. On the next morning, December 11th, they set off again, stopped for dinner 2 miles north of George's Bayou, and reached Old St.

Andrews at 5:00 PM. What a strange sight it must have been for George's friends to see the pink urchins on the bay shore.

On December 12th George immediately went to work on the place, planting and trimming trees, and putting out bulbs and roses. The next day the group went by steam yacht to Hurricane Island, and the day after to Harmon's Bayou, the northern arm of Massalina Bayou. Capt. Lambert Ware, Sr. came to call on George and his friends.

December 15th George left the Bay, stopped again just north of Georges Bayou and reached Econfina at 6:00 PM, finding all as he had left it in the spring – "unchanged and unchangeable" he wrote. He set off from Econfina at 8:00 AM the next morning and arrived in Marianna at 7:30 PM. The ride that day was difficult in a pouring rain. In Marianna he roamed around for the day, gathering mistletoe and violets in wooded areas. December 19th, 4 days after leaving the Bay, he arrived in Chicago.

George arrived home in time to act the part of Santa Claus for Wixon's store on the 24th. The Wests celebrated Christmas on the 25th this year, having their tree and exchanging gifts that day. A set of shirt buttons, gold chain, and a knife were George's gifts.

December 30th A cloudy day and threatening snow – Feel listless and disappointed – Mrs. Scott takes dinner with us – called at Mr. T's this evening – Home early and to bed – aweary aweary. Commenced snowing about 8:30 Wind SE. How the ice creaks and groans tonight – as though a thousand caged spirits straining to break their icy bonds and rend asunder the Fort Kings shackles – Alas too late – The bonds are too strongly forged –

December 31st Awake to find the storm still raging furiously – 8 inches of snow already fallen – Trains late – All day the snow comes down - covering deeply all semblance of roads – paths or shrubs - every house has its cornice of white while the gateposts stand like whitecapped sentries by untrodden paths. What a wealth of snow – How pure – How picturesque – Yes as I stroll along the street in the twilight it seems really beautiful to me – Is it so, or is it because I look at it through cheerful eyes – The old year is fast passing away – I am less gloomy than I was a year ago tonight. It has been a year of hard work to me – but there have been joys as well as trials – and a bright sky comes to me with the New Year – That which was but a hope a year ago – a wish for a southern home – has become a reality. The silent hopes of this evening – will they too come in the future to be so real? Take it all in all 1887 has been kind to me – May 1888 be no less so.

1888

The year opened with George already planning to return to St. Andrews. He conducted his railroad business as usual in the harsh winter weather, did some sleigh riding, and had his "blue" days often. On February 6th he set out by train for Chicago, and there met up with his son Charles and new daughter-in-law Eleanor "Nellie" Brown West. The Brown family owned about 120 acres of the Squaw Point land, minus 1 acre sold to the government for a lighthouse.

In Chicago he purchased some hammocks for the house at St. Andrews. That evening they set off on the train and arrived in Nashville the next morning. A train wreck in a tunnel between Nashville and Birmingham held up the train for 12 hours and delayed their arrival in Montgomery until 2:00PM on the 8th. In Montgomery they rented 2 carriages and toured the town until the train was ready to leave for Marianna. The group finally made it to Marianna, stayed overnight, and set out for St. Andrews with 3 teams and wagons at 8:00 AM on February 10th. The going was slow due to heavy rain and they did not arrive at Gainer until 8:15 PM. After resting overnight, they again set out and reached St. Andrews at 3:45 PM on February 11th. This trip had taken 6 days of travel. They found the house in good shape, the hyacinths and tulips in bloom. George took a team up town to St. Andrews and got a stove, mattresses, and provisions. They celebrated that night with supper in the new house including radishes from his garden. Charles and Nellie took the bedroom downstairs, George and Dell took the unfinished bedroom upstairs, and he wrote that it was like camping out.

The next few days were spent getting the place in shape. There was much to clean up in the house and yard, and they received a basket of chickens from Econfina. George and Charles cleared the lot and around the spring, put up the hammocks, and enjoyed those in the pleasant evening. George set up a dark room in "the old house", an additional structure on the property.

February 22nd Cloudy – sultry – about 78 in the shade all day – went out with gun this forenoon. Laid in hammock long time this noon – hoed in garden this PM. Peas, lettuce – parsnips – beets – Radishes – Potatoes – Carrots – Mustards – all up and doing nicely. Hoed them all out – somewhat lonesome today.

February 28th Bright nice day. We secure Ware's boat and go to Land's End. Reach there about 1 – nice ride. Wixon shoots some gulls and I one. Get about two bushels shells. Start home at 4, calm at 5 and row the boat around the Point. Breeze freshens and at 8 we are home. All enjoying it very much.

February 29ᵗʰ Nice day. Get away for Masselena's Point this forenoon for pictures. Lovely ride over and an elegant day for pictures. Took 15. Home early and all enjoyed ride....Carpenter at work.

March 1ˢᵗ Fixing up negatives – and getting ends & c (and such) in readiness for packing this forenoon – Printed some pictures today – about 5 PM commenced packing – very nice day. To bed about 9:20. The last day on pleasant St. Andrews Bay – Carpenter at work on verandah.

On March 2ⁿᵈ George left the pleasant bay and Dell, and headed north in a rig, along with Charles and Nellie. Along the way George picked violets and other wild flowers in the woods. The party stopped at 4:00 in the afternoon at Econfina, George took pictures, and they spent the night. The next morning he picked strawberries, bid farewell to Econfina and wondered would he ever see his old plantation again. He wrote to Dell from Econfina, Montgomery, and all along the route home by train.

Nellie and Charles West at a spring on the Econfina, most likely Gainer Spring where they stopped often, GMW Collection, BCPL

They arrived home in Escanaba on March 5th, having made much better time than the trip down. Escanaba was draped in ice, snow, and had a ferocious gale blowing. Trouble with tracks in poor condition because of the freezing demanded George's immediate attention. In April a tug was still needed to break the ice on the bay so the ships cold get in the harbor and to the port docks. Finally in June, George was able to put on "thin underclothing" and Dell returned home. She was ill most of June.

In July George's friend Chris Peterson was ill and dying. It was imminent.

July 15th A cloudy day – Feel very blue. Try to sleep away the time. I tire of life such days as this ands the night – Ah that it had never come to me – Along long walk this evening – alone – alone - visit Chris. He is forthgoing – would that I were in his place.

Then within a couple of days George's state of mind was changed and he marveled at the evening.

July 19th ...A bright beautiful evening – moonlight perfect - and the air as balmy as the night is glorious - The delicate perfume of new mown hay from the hay fields – this aromatic laden air from the balsams and spruces – the evening moon set in a circle of brilliant coloring - the racing of the deer upon the hill...what a night.

Highlights in the remainder of the year included the return of the circus, a lunar eclipse George studied as it happened, and hunting in the fall with Charles. In November George oversaw more than 24,000 tons of ore run out of the dock between 7:00 AM and 6:00 PM in one day. Work matters had to be drawn to a close before the bay froze over.

The end of November brought the family what George called a *"cheerful evening, but a thread of sorrow is woven in ...with the joy."* In a difficult labor, Nellie had given birth to Philip Brown West and then the doctor had to come and operate to *"relieve her of her last child",* Ernest Warren West. The twin of Philip only lived a couple of days and was buried in Escanaba on November 29th, one day after George's 43rd birthday.

December 31st ....Feel so gloomy this evening but the day closes with more happiness than I anticipated.... And thus ends 1888. A busy year for me and ours that has taken much of my vitality to get through – No one year has ever been so hard on me physically. It has been the greatest years business that the Peninsula Division ever had – and been so successful in every way as could have been desired. Financially I have gained somewhat and the prospects for the future in this respect seems brighter – There have been troubles to overcome and grief – but there has been joy also – hours of perfect happiness – which have gone far too assuage troubles wounds – The silent thoughts of a year ago – slowly they frame themselves in to form – the form takes on semblances and hope points cheerfully to the future and bids me be content. May 1889 bring naught to mar this picture – nothing to disappoint and grieve me. Shall be happiness and joy.

1889

The routine of work in the cold winter kept George busy as he also made plans to return to St. Andrews in February. He enjoyed another celestial show on the 5th when he saw a *"beautiful meteor in the southwest at 7:15 PM. As large as a puck ...as light as day".* When not working he continued his photography, taking pictures of baby Philip and rooms in the house.

February 4th the Wests and a group of friends set off on the train headed south. He chose a different route this time, taking the train into Mobile, Alabama. There he visited some friends and took photographs of the camellia shrubs in their yard and picked an armful for himself.

Camellias, GMW Collection, BCPL

On February 7th the party boarded a ship and left the dock at 9:00 AM. They headed out Mobile Bay and into the Gulf of Mexico passing by Fort Morgan, Alabama. There George spotted the stack of the *USS Tecumseh*. The 223' Union ship had been in the Battle of Mobile Bay during the Civil War and struck a mine that sank it on August 5, 1864. At dusk the St. Andrews bound party was just off Pensacola and George turned in for the night at 8:30 PM. At 2:00 AM the ship was laying off the East Pass into St. Andrews Bay and the captain was waiting for daylight before he proceeded into St. Andrews Bay. They arrived at Ware's Dock at 8:45 AM and walked down to the house. George found everything in good order.

George immediately went to work on unpacking and cleaning up the yard. Most of the days were fairly warm and moist. Rainy days kept him in the house so he read books or wrote to Charles and friends back in Escanaba. George built a dock during this time as he planned for a boat of his own. After about 10 days of dock building in between rain showers, George took a trip to Watsons Bayou successfully hunting quail with Thomas Gwaltney. He also struck a friendship with Narcisco "Hawk" Massalina. George used a variety of spellings when writing Hawk's last name in the diaries.

Hawk Massalina and Adella West, GMW Collection, BCPL

February 23rd A clear nice day – no boat so can't go anywhere – Finished the dock today – Thomas at the house – Saw Hawk. He is to come Monday. Bought some lumber for the dock ...

February 24th A clear warm day – went out in woods at noon – took couple pictures this PM. Wrote everyone – picked some peach blossoms and Ti Ti – Fine PM and coat off writing in my diary.

February 25th 52 degrees, cloudy. Partly cloudy day – Hawk over at 6:30 am. Went to Wileys – took pictures – then to Hurricane – got shells. Home at 6:30 Pm. Nice days work.

February 26th 56 degrees, clear. A very nice day. Hawk over at 11 and all go over to his point – took 8 pictures. Shot a pelican going over. Very large one 4 ft 6 bill to tail extreme length. 7 ft 6 from tip to tip wing. Developed pictures until 12 at night. Some very nice ones. Set out oranges.

February 28th ended George's time in St. Andrews for this trip. March 6th he was back in Escanaba again and all was well at home. His expenses to travel south this time had cost $46.80, including the overnight stay in Mobile. The return trip was $20.90 total including the wagon to Marianna to catch the train.

In Escanaba spring once again found him feeling blue and he wrote "...*The rain falls pitilessly this evening – would that it was falling on my grave. Rain rain – In joy and adversity*". He longed to return to St. Andrews and wrote "*I feel fairly well – but my mind takes me far away – to more congenial skies*".

In June the King-Franklin Circus came to Escanaba. It had only been established in 1888 and featured an extravagant Wild West Show, complete with cowboys and cowgirls dancing the Virginia Reel. The Wests and friends enjoyed this show, Sunday School picnics, and also going out to baseball games in the evenings during the summer. While setting off the July 4th fireworks for the city George burned his arm when one of the explosives burst close to him. Later in the summer George built a small boat for use on the nearby pond and river. He had a constant thirst to learn about so many topics and he purchased a book on yachting. He launched his new little boat in August and was pleased with the performance in the water. George wrote often to his new friends Capt. Ware, Hawk, and others in St. Andrews and also sent pictures to them.

Philip Brown West, in Escanaba, Michigan, GMW Collection, BCPL

December 31st ...And with a gale of wind from the southland ends 1889 – Many precious hours has it given me – many – but not so many as of the above – of very very sorrowful ones – Would that 1890 could be all that I picture for it and that no ill may come to me or mine is my earnest wish – I am better physically than a year ago – the year's work has not worn on me as did 1888. In a business way I have been fairly successful and laid by a trifle. On the road over 3,000,000 tons have been moved and a wonderful record made. May 1890 be no worse – and may I avoid the faults – the troubles of 1889.

1890

January was filled with making sure the railroad office was in order, George having an extensive amount of dental work, and getting ready to go south to St. Andrews. For unknown reason George wrote he had no interest in making this trip.

On February 5th the small party left on the train and only required a single and a double rig when setting out from Marianna. They stopped overnight at McAllister's place on Bear Creek. This became a regular stop for George. February 10th they arrived at St. Andrews at 11:40 AM. After surveying the property and finding everything in good shape and his plants growing, George headed up town to Ware's and the Post Office. He saw Hawk and others and did some catching up.

On his first full day at the bay this visit, George went to an oyster bed in the bay and before noon had picked up 500 oysters. Hawk brought him sharks heads and fish heads. Heading up town for his usual walk to the post office, George encountered Mr. Hoffman going to the beach so George joined him on the vessel *Flying Dutchman*. At Gulf Beach George took photographs of the dunes and surf. The next day they went freshwater fishing and George landed 4 nice bass. The vessel *Nettie* came in to Ware's dock on the 15th and the Wests' trunks were on board. George got those home and unpacked. Capt. and Mrs. Sheppard, Col. and Mrs. Doty, the Brackins, and Lt. and Mrs. Gwaltney often called on the West family in the evenings. Days were often spent going over to Hurricane Island and Lands End to hunt, gather crabs, and pick up shells.

February 19th 60 degrees, clear. A nice morning – Hawk over and we all start for East Bay points – Shoot 3 pelicans during the day. Visit Cromanton. Saw peaches growing size of large walnuts. From

49

Cromanton to Watson Bayou a beautiful bayou – visited Mrs. Holmes place. Lunch on point at mouth Bayou. Then up East bay as far as Parker then home. Cloudy – wind south – Only been home a short time when Dave came with boat to go fire fishing. Start at 5 – nearly 9 when we get to the lagoon. Fishing good – Get wood and keep it up all night.

February 20th 60 degrees, clear. Light southwest wind – fished until about 4:30 am – then for home – arrived at 6 – a fine night spent – 64 fish. Redfish 4-6- pounds each – mullet – sheepsheads – flounders – chofers – blowfish – trout – Oyster fish – and crabs. Took pictures of flounder and redfish this am... Capt. Sheppard was down to give me a sail – Blowing half a gale from SouthW. Went to PO and back... To bed 10:15. Developed 3 negatives.

The 2-masted sailboat directly behind the mail boat was the *Jerome L. Rogers*, owned by Hawk Massalina, GMW Collection, BCPL

Hawk came to the West home regularly and took folks up town and to other points on the bay in his boat. On February 27th in a gale blowing from the southeast, George, Hawk, and Mr. Miller set out at 9:00 AM for Crooked Island. They stopped at noon on Hurricane Island. The wind was strong and *"a big sea running in the passes"*. Capt. Ware came after them, reaching the island at the same time. The party ventured on toward Crooked Island taking quite a pounding and a thorough wetting. They arrived at Crooked Island by evening, set up the tent, and cooked supper. They woke the next morning at 5:30, the wind still blowing hard, and they struck camp, boarded Hawk's boat, and headed for Goose Bayou. Just 2 tacks in the small sailboat took them to their destination. At Goose Bayou they cooked breakfast and were able get some game, a duck and a bird. The southeast wind blew in the rain and they quickly boarded the boat to head for home. At 10:00 AM the small boat was in Crooked Island pass when a squall struck them and before they could reef (lower) the mainsail, the wind split the sail. It was 6:00 PM before the party made it to the Wests' dock and the wind had shifted from the north.

George's chosen route to return to Escanaba was again by boat. The going in the Gulf of Mexico was slow and cold with a southwest wind beating against the side of the boat. Cold and wet, George got in his berth fully clothed at 5:00 PM but it was midnight before he was comfortable. It was midnight the next evening before they reached Pensacola. There George bought some things for baby Philip, got his trunk to the depot and boarded the northbound train. The train stopped over in Nashville where George got off and visited the State Capital. There he read the account of Capt. Robinson and his Confederate army's fight against the Union's vessel *Roebuck* at Old Town. The account later became George's information used to write and publish "The Skirmish at Old Town St. Andrews, Fla." in 1918. Upon arrival at Evansville, Indiana on March 6th, George found the Ohio River was flooded and "miles wide". Houses and trees were all underwater and he photographed the scene from his window on the train.

Flooded town of Evansville, GMW Collection, BCPL

He arrived in Chicago on March 7th and there he got a shave, had dinner, and went to the Chicago & North Western Railroad General office. Total expenses for this return trip had cost him $13.75. He mailed pictures and wrote to the Dotys, Sheppards, Dell, and others. George took the opportunity to visit an exhibit of Madeleine Lemaire. She was a French painter in oils and watercolors, flowers, particularly roses, being her subject of choice. Her enormous success during her lifetime earned her being called the "Empress of Roses".

March 26th 32 degrees. Snowed little this am then cleared away and thawed some but very cold north wind. Very much out of patience this PM. Everything goes wrong. Read this evening Explorations in Africa – to bed 9:30.

Springtime came and Scarlet Fever struck Escanaba. The West family was spared but baby Philip was ill with a bad stomach for several days. Dell remained in St. Andrews until summer. Charles went to Chicago in April and ordered a boat for George. The boat arrived July 15th, a day before the 25th wedding anniversary of George and Dell. He tried out the new boat several times on the bay at Escanaba and in a few weeks packed it again and loaded it into a freight car to be shipped to St. Andrews. On August 3rd George tried out riding a bicycle for the first time.

On December 11th George, Dell, Charles, Nellie and 2 year old Philip set out for St. Andrews by train. Taking yet a different route, they arrived in New Orleans on the 12th. They visited the Lafayette House, the French Market, and took a 3 mile train ride out St. Charles Street to see the "fine" residences there. At 3:15 PM they started for Chipley in what George described as an awfully old sleeper car. The train arrived in Chipley the next morning at 9:00 and George hired rigs for the trip to St. Andrews. They spent the night along the Econfina and made it to St. Andrews the next day at 2:45 PM. George found everything looking better than he expected, got the trunks in, and unpacked some.

The next morning he got his old row boat from the ways but found a small hole slice in one side. He got it rigged up and operational so he could use it until his new boat arrived. The wind was blowing strong for several days, but he finally was able to make a trip over to Redfish Point to see Hawk and gather some lemons there. He continued to work around his property trimming trees and cleaning up. George went in the boat to the saw mill and ordered lumber for walks and a chicken coop, and he purchased some nails. He went back when the lumber was to be ready and loaded as much as he could into his small boat. Then he and Charles set to work building the first of the walks around the property. Another day they built the hen coop then started back on building the walks.

In front of the house, showing the front porch, the old red cedar, the roses, cactus, young palm, yucca, and the woods across the run. In

West home on St. Andrews Bay with boardwalks George was constructing around the property, BCPL

In time for Christmas George's new boat arrived from Escanaba by train into Pensacola, then was transferred to a ship and brought to St. Andrews. Hawk took the boat when it was unloaded and brought it to George's dock on the 24th. The family's Christmas tree that evening was a little yaupon from the shoreline of St. Andrews Bay. They decorated the rest of the house with more yaupon, palm leaves, palmettos, Spanish bayonet, moss, and cedar. George also picked a vase full of roses from his garden. The next few days George and Charles successfully hunted and the family enjoyed duck for dinner. The nights were growing colder and he wrapped up his bananas on the trees.

Hawk came on the 30th and the men all set off for Crooked Island to hunt. They camped overnight sleeping in the sand on the north peninsula of Crooked Island, and returned home at 5:15 PM on New Years Eve.

December 31st ...Thus ends 1890. A very busy year – It finds me under southern skies – A strange New Years clime to one used to the cold of January.

1891

George closed out his first New Years day in the southland by negotiating a deal with Thomas Gwaltney. For a year, Thomas was to take charge of the house and use the garden and George was to pay him $10 per month. The next few days George and Charles spent hunting in the daytime and fire fishing at night, getting ducks, redfish, sheepshead, snapper, mullet, flounder, drum, and chofers.

They also found someone to haul lumber and continued the work on building the walks. Capt. Lambert Ware took them over to Spanish Shanty Cove to hunt one morning. There, in the freezing January weather, George saw the most "immense" water moccasin he had ever seen.

By January 27th George, Charles, Nellie and Philip were back in Escanaba. Dell had travelled as far as Birmingham and remained there with friends until the 31st.

Springtime brought more joy to the family. Nellie gave birth to Grace Hughwitt West at 2:30 AM on April 5th. Charles went for the nurse, and while he was gone, with only Dell on hand, Grace had been born quietly and quickly. George and Dell began to spend more time taking Philip for walks and such, giving Nellie time to care for her newborn.

George sold his interest in the *Jane Anderson* on April 22nd to Capt. Hewlett. He then turned his attention to work and gardening, putting out hollyhocks, pansies, asters, and mulching his roses. He had some carpenters add on to the house in Escanaba and on June 27th carpet was laid. July 1st the masons finished the chimney in the kitchen, and stairs and a library were added.

As customary George was to set off the city's July 4th fireworks. A cluster of rockets exploded, throwing the heads in all directions and setting everything on fire. George and his helper jumped into the water with minor injuries. There ended the night's display.

The next day sad news was given to George. Charles was diagnosed with an illness and it was terminal. Most likely it was tuberculosis. Charles was on a special diet to try and help his condition and he tired of the diet quickly.

Charles Ernest West, GMW Collection, BCPL

July 5th Clear – high north wind – cool – a quiet day after the 4th. I am blue and tonight Dr. T called me out for a walk and told me of Charles' condition. What a terrible blow to me – My boy – my companion – the only one – to be taken from me by this horrible disease – I cannot sleep or bear to be awake.

Both work and daily life demanded George's attention. The family spent time boating and George ordered another boat this time from New York. George sold as much of his property in Escanaba as he could and sent the balance of $650.00 due for the boat.

The family headed back to St. Andrews on December 10th taking the train down to Pensacola. From there the large party on this trip boarded a ship, left the Pensacola dock at 6:55 AM, and arrived at Ware's dock at 6:30 that evening. The weather was rough on the ride over and all were sick but Nellie, Charles, Philip, and George.

The weather stayed cloudy, rainy, and windy, but George got his new launch *Gladys* in the water and took a ride with Frank and Capt. Ware along. He went uptown in the boat most days to the post office and he purchased naptha for the boat at Ware's. There was little else to do in these few days other than read and work around inside the house.

Gladys on St. Andrews Bay, GMW Collection, BCPL

The family had their Christmas on the 24th with a nice tree and George received 2 ties. The next day he planted Confederate Jasmine and some seeds, and the family had a turkey dinner.

December 31st 51 degrees, Partly cloudy. Clearing toward noon – Start at 9 for North Bay. Go as far as Gays Mill on east side – then start for West Bay – Go in to Burnt Mill Creek... about sundown start for home – good run and make it at 7. Quiet. Conclude to go firefishing tonight. Get off at 8:15 fishing by 9:30. Wind begins to freshen in Lagoon. Stay until 12 but wind is so bad cannot do anything after 10 – Got 11. Redfish. Trout - Sheepshead and mullet. Start home – lose small boat about 1 mile out of lagoon by line breaking. Sea runs high. Go back after it. Find it ok. Go to Ware's Point before find we are on wrong course. Home about 2 AM. 1st launch behaved nicely in the sea – wind coming up strong from SE. New year finds me at the Lagoon.

1892

The winter weather made this visit to St. Andrews frustrating. Northwest winds at a gale, rain, some snow and sleet, and colder temperatures kept George from doing much hunting or fishing for several days. He only managed to take a few short boat rides with friends along. They took a hunting trip into West Bay and Burnt Mill Creek, but a heavy fog moved in before they could get home. They steered with a little compass which they read by the light of cigars. Once they hit land on the east side of West Bay, George and Charles gathered lighter-wood on the shore and used the lit pieces to follow the shoreline to home where they arrived at 9:30 PM.

The *Nettie* came in to Ware's carrying the mattresses and a chair for Philip that George had purchased. He and Charles planted trees on the property. The varieties included Satsuma Orange, several plum varieties, White Adriatic Fig, and peach trees. After a few more days of socializing with friends, boating, and taking tea, George headed back to Escanaba on January 27th. He and Thomas Gwaltney renewed their agreement for Thomas to take charge of the place for another year and George agreed to pay him $10 a month.

Upon return to Escanaba George found the water pipes in the house had frozen. It took 2 men 2 days to repair the plumbing. He tended to his railroad work but took time to view the occultation of Venus and Jupiter, and also went to Dr. Booth's and looked in his microscope.

March 4th he headed back to St. Andrews. After getting off the train at Chipley, he hired a hack to take him to Bear Creek where Charles was waiting with the *Gladys*. The naptha-run boat got them to George's dock in 3 hours 25 minutes.

Though the March winds were blowing most days, he took the family for leisurely outings on the boat to Gulf Beach and Land's End where they gathered scallops and shells.

George had to start back toward Escanaba on March 14th and Charles took him by boat back to Bear Creek. The ride to Chipley had already left, so George and Charles camped overnight. The next morning the team showed up at 11:00 and George made it in time to catch the train in Chipley.

In Escanaba, George was thrust into work as the season was opening. Many days he missed meals. Dell, Charles, Nellie and the children returned to Escanaba in May. By June Charles' illness was taking over his body. July 19th George and Charles took the train to Chicago. Charles enjoyed the change of scenery and the train ride in the twilight. The pair spent time going to the circus, to the World's Fair grounds, and to the theatre to see *Ali Baba*. Towards the end of July George could only sit by.

July 25th   Thunder showers since mid-night. C (Charles) very weak this AM and drowsy. Not up when I came down – all through the day he was drowsy, but not hard to awaken – his will is indominitable.

July 26th   A warm day. C slept all night but it was more a stupor than sleep – I went in to his room several times to see if he was alright. At noon he would come downstairs and walked down quite strong – I dressed him as he wished to be to see callers. He failed fast this afternoon – at 6 he is suffering terribly for health and appeals so piteously to me for help. The end is near – Drs Booth and Reynolds try to help him but without avail – at 1 he is easier – for death is near – Oh what an afternoon of suffering for him and all...

July 27th   Oh how long it seems to day light – I sit by Charlie holding his hand in my own and he is slowly passing away – About 6 I thought he was going and burst into tears – He looks in to my eyes with a sweet smile and gives me his hand – what a satisfaction is this – He has not felt his sufferings much since 12 – At 9:47 today my idol – my only companion – breathes his last. Oh how can I bear it – How bravely he met his death – How courageous to the end – Make preparations to bury him at Brandon Friday – Friends all notified.

The next morning a service was held for Charles in Escanaba at 7:00 AM and representatives from all the railroad lodges attended. George wrote that the flowers were very pretty and Charles looked restful. The family left by train at 7:55 and accompanied the body to Brandon, Wisconsin for burial at the Brandon Cemetery. The casket was $50, the doctor bill was $13, and the hearse and miscellaneous expenses was $12. George paid $36 for 4 more plots, those being the ones that would eventually hold the remains of Charles, Ernest, Nellie, and Adella. Many old friends were awaiting the Wests at the cemetery.

The next day George called for Dr. Booth to come see Dell. She had been prostrate since Charles' passing and was suffering from her old pains also. George wrote that *"It seems as though life were unworthy living. After all our struggle, Charles & I to get things as we would like them – he must be taken just when* (all) *was at hand"*. George spent the evening picking out negatives of Charles. In the weeks to come everything reminded George of his loss. He was lonely and heartbroken. Dell remained ill for weeks.

CHICAGO & NORTH-WESTERN RAILWAY CO.

OFFICE OF GENERAL SUPERINTENDENT

CHICAGO,   Aug. 12, 1892.   D

Mr. G. M. West,

     Asst.Supt., Pen.Div., Escanaba.

     My Dear Sir:-

          I am in receipt of your letter of Aug. 8th. There will be no bill sent to you from the St.Paul Ry. for running the special train that you refer to.

     I want to extend to you my heartfelt sympathy for you and your family in the loss of your son.

     Yours truly,

     Gen.supt.

George had to press forward with work and tried to pursue his hobbies. He escorted on a hike to Pine Ridge 2 professors from the Agricultural College who were in search of botanical specimens. He also continued his photography work, but wrote *"Life seems to have lost all there is in it to me"*.

Nellie received $4,000.00 from Charles' life insurance policy, but George disagreed with her choice of where she deposited it. He wrote that he would have a talk with her about the investment of her money, when the time was right. George purchased a desk for Philip, who was now 4, and he ordered bulbs for St. Andrews, even though he felt life was not worth living.

The first of November George packed 2 boxes for shipment by train to St. Andrews, and he took up 25 roses which he sent by mail. In early December both Philip and Grace were ill, but all were preparing to return to St. Andrews. They arrived on December 9th to the place looking very well with roses in bloom and trees having grown. Dell was still sick and remained in bed at the house. Hawk brought George's boats over to the dock and George rowed the *Gladys* to Ware's store for naptha. The engine fired right up. He tended to fixing up things in the house and hanging curtains, and in a few days managed to get Dell out for a boat ride. She ended up right back in bed.

George and Hawk went to Harmons Bayou to hunt, getting duck and dove. That about used all the naptha George had been able to get at Ware's and he waited each day for the *Nettie* to arrive with more.

The Christmas Eve tree and house trimming delighted the children and everyone had presents. George received a rule, fur slippers, cake soap, and a book. The temperature was 68 and was perfect for lying out in the hammock in the evening. The next day George attempted flash light photography for the first time. He used up all his developing material and had one good and one bad picture.

December 31ˢᵗ ...By 10 the tide is up to the dock and running over it. Tide is higher than ever I saw it tonight and a gale as hard as I have seen it – About midnight it shifts to west and rains at the turn of the storm – so ends the year with a gale that shakes the house and roars on the beach – and so tired I cannot keep awake.

1893

The *Nettie* came in and George was able to secure 30 gallons of naptha for his launch. The party all went by boat to the beach at Hurricane Island and gathered shells, and also took a boat ride to Cromanton. George continued work on the walks at the house and did some hunting with Hawk. No luck hunting, but they gathered a sack of oysters. Cold and windy days kept them in the house some. January 9ᵗʰ the men went to West Bay to hunt and got caught up in a gale. They started for home at 5:15 PM but had to anchor the boat in a protected spot. Some went ashore and built a fire waiting for the wind to fall. George laid down in the boat and slept until 9:15 PM. Once underway again, they made it home at 11:10 PM with their 24 birds from the hunt.

George was feeling very well the next day but the wind kept him indoors hugging the fire. So he ordered 18 more trees including 7 peaches, 1 apricot, 1 nectarine, 1 mulberry, 1 almond, 1 black walnut, 1 pecan, 2 plums, an English walnut, and others. Hawk came over and they talked of going cooing for dove. The next day after dinner George and Will Look went to Hawk's point and indeed the hunting was successful. The sea was running quite strong and the wind picked up again. George noted in his diary the wind *"blows right through the house"*. He hired Hawk to caulk seams and cracks in front of the house.

The wind and cold finally broke and the party was able to go boating over to Hawk's then to Spanish Shanty cove for an outing. Then George got a little gardening done, and all but Nellie went to Hurricane Island for a day. The bay was smooth, the air warmer, and lots of fine shells were collected. Fire fishing, boat rides, and beautiful sunsets were enjoyed by all for the next few days. George also took the wash across the bay to Hawk's.

West Home on St. Andrews Bay, BCPL

The house was painted, George put out scuppernongs, fertilized the trees, settled up his account with Capt. Ware, and got ready for his trip north. January 29th he was on a railroad once more. Some of his expenses were: sleeper to Pensacola .50, supper .50, sleeper Pensacola to Montgomery 1.50, haircut and shave .50, breakfast .75, day car to Nashville 1.50, dinner .75, supper .75, and Chicago sleeper 2.50.

February 1st ...Seems as though I had only been out of the office a day or so. Cannot imagine I have had my holiday and am to wait a year for another – Found all well at the house –

George was thrust back into the daily railroad work in nasty weather that was 5 to 20 degrees below zero every night. The brutal cold brought on aches and pains throughout his body. He wrote and submitted an article for Outing magazine. Outing was established in 1882 and was printed until 1923. It featured outdoor recreation, sports, and travel. No record of an article by George has been found.

In George's papers was a copy of a bill passed on June 3rd, 1893 by the State of Florida authorizing the incorporation of the Florida Grand Trunk Railway Company, and their acquisition of lands and construction standards to build a railroad into the panhandle of Florida. George was not a named party in this corporation, but he already had interest in the construction of rail to the St. Andrews Bay area.

May 27th Dell, Nellie, and the children returned to Escanaba. Accompanying them was Capt. Lambert Ware, Sr. and his 12-year-old son Lambert "Bert" Ware to pay a visit to George for a few days. The summer was difficult for George as the loss of Charles the previous summer was remembered.

In August and September he spent a great deal of time in Chicago at the World's Columbian Exposition. The Exposition was a World's fair to celebrate the 400th anniversary of Christopher Columbus' arrival in the new World. There George saw the Machinery building, Manufacturing, Fine Arts, Costa Rica exhibit, Forestry building, and Wild West show. He visited the California and Illinois displays, and the mining building that featured precious stones. Together he and Dell took in the art and Anthropological exhibits and saw the electrical light display and show for the first time.

George did not write much in his diary for 3 weeks but what he did write was that he thought he would discontinue his diary.

On December 12th George and the family boarded the train to head back to St. Andrews. Philip was sick and the doctor called upon in Pensacola said it was diphtheria. The family had to remain in Pensacola until December 22nd when Philip was improving and able to travel on to St. Andrews. They were able to get to St. Andrews before Christmas and found everything in good shape. Hawk brought the *Gladys* over to the dock for the family. He had used and cared for it during George's absence and was paid $15. Christmas was quiet with Dell sick and young Philip still weak from his illness.

December 31st Clearing away today – cooler – All about same. Dell taken this PM with terrible pain in her head and face – could not get anything to relieve it – I feel weak and cough badly – Clear but cool night – This closes 1893 a year that has been fruitful in disappointments to me – I am glad it is over.

1894

The entire family started out 1894 with an illness, or weak from being ill. For several days they did little but rest. After a week the weather was mild and comfortable and everyone must have had cabin fever. They took some nice outings in the boat to Smack Bayou, Watson Bayou, and Land's End. Then George got down to business working on his trees and garden. He also began a sketch of the property and plantings, which became his map of "The Palms". This map showed buildings, trees, garden area, walks, and such on his property. He also worked on construction of a boat hoist at the end of his dock and completed it on January 19th. On the 20th a gale blew and the water rose high up the beach. He was unable to get the *Gladys* on the hoist until it slacked up some and when he did hoist her, found that there were 2 or 3 holes from the bow smashing onto a sunken piling. The boat was repaired and some more gardening work completed before George went north on the 27th. He arrived back in Escanaba on February 2nd.

Dell also kept a diary at this time while in St. Andrews. She kept busy at baking bread, mending, going for the mail, and helping with house work. She helped Nellie with the children, watched them while Nellie took a bath, sewed for Philip, and gave him a bath. They took boat rides with Hawk, took the children to the park, and had friends join them for lunch.

By March 24th George headed back to St. Andrews meeting up with his friend Mr. Pillsbury in Pensacola, who joined him on the trip. Capt. Frank Ware, brother of Capt. Lambert Ware, Sr., met them at the train in Chipley on the 25th and they set off for St. Andrews in a single rig. George marveled at the wild flowers in bloom in the woods and by the wayside. In St. Andrews George found all quiet and well at home. After a couple of mornings of frost and chilly temperatures, they were able to set out in the *Gladys* on some excursions to Hawk's, Watson Bayou, and Parker. While at Spanish Shanty Cove on one of the boat rides Dell lost a ring in the cove. Nellie was getting out socializing more and attended a dance in St. Andrews.

March 31st A clear morning and calm... Will go to bear Creek – took in 10 gal naptha and getting Pillsbury – Strait for Ware's dock at 9 AM. All the folks but Nellie and Grace. Reach the mouth of Cedar Creek at 11:30 and 12:30 at Indian Bluff where we took our lunch. Then explored the Econfina for some miles – A picturesque spot. Then up the Cedar Creek 2 miles – Then for home at 4. Reach there little after 7 – Got ready to go fire fishing – and over to the lagoon at 9 PM. Too low water – Stay until 2 AM – home a little after 3 AM...

April 2nd George was back on the rails to Escanaba. Dell, Nellie, and the children remained in St. Andrews. Intermingled with his railroad work

George spent a lot of time with his gardening, in the conservatory, and taking groups by train to go wild flower picking. He went to Wixon's Studio and photographed the hepaticas flowers. He had a printing plate made and this photograph was used in his published leaflet about the plant and in the Panama City Pilot edition about gardening on April 22nd, 1909.

GMW Collection, BCPL

Dell, Nellie, and the children returned to Escanaba in late May, accompanied this year by Col. Doty. Coming up on the anniversary of Charles' death George pondered *"three years ago Charles and I went over the same ground at the same time of the year and it all came back to me. It was the last of our outings"*. George busied himself writing up his Hepaticas booklet and photographing other plants. On the railroad there was another strike and George was sent to Milwaukee to work on switching cars in the yard. He and Will Look handled switching 186 cars in a day. The striking switchmen were picketing and called George and Will "scabs". He returned to Escanaba that night and found 26 men to send to Milwaukee the next morning and wrote in his diary *"Chicago still in hands of mob"*.

Once the strike was settled George spent some time with his close friends William Hatten, Col. Doty, and Will Look. Late July through August was a particularly blue time for George possibly because it was the time of year when both his father and son died. Dell's recurring illness most likely did not help.

August 30th 60 degrees. All days are alike – I feel melancholy and everything conspires to keep me so – Dell about same – The medicine does not seem to help her...Feel so blue and tormented by every thought...What grief the heart can bear and not break...

The doctor was making efforts to help Dell, giving her "hot water injections" and "washing out her stomach", but she showed no improvement. One of her diagnosis was pleurisy, the inflammation of the membrane around her lungs. Caused possibly by a virus, the damage was permanent and caused her to have pain especially when breathing.

This quiet Christmas was spent in Escanaba. George was unsure of when to leave for St. Andrews, but finally packed a trunk and they set off on New Years Eve.

1895

In Pensacola they waited for the boat that would take them to St. Andrews. George passed the time attending a football game between the Memphis Athletic Club and the Pensacola Club, Memphis winning 24 to 0. He also purchased supplies, trees, and plants for the house in St. Andrews. Nellie and little Grace passed the time visiting Fort Barrancas in Pensacola, Florida. After 10 days the boat finally arrived and the large party for St. Andrews got underway by the light of a full moon.

At his home in St. Andrews the winter winds were blowing and prevented any hunting or fishing, so George worked around the house and yard. He tied up the roses and honeysuckle, got lumber to build onto the chicken pen, and hung pictures and curtains. Nellie attended a party. By January 18th the wind had fallen off enough to take the party out on the boat. They got away from Ware's dock at 1:45 PM with Aunt Sarah, Mrs. Hall, Mamie, Edna, Nellie, Grace, Hattie, Capt. Ware, Mr. Williford, and Otway (9 year old son of Capt. Lambert Ware, Sr.), going towards Bay Head. A fine ride and nice location to tarry was found. The party arrived back at the West dock at 8:30 PM.

The next few days George spent finishing the chicken coop, and just in time as some chickens and ducks he ordered from Pensacola arrived on a steamer January 24th. He continued with his gardening and cleaning up the property. Dell was having an ill spell. George paid taxes on his boat, and was outraged that its value was assessed at $500. He planted seeds and cleaned up around the Governor Clark monument just west of his home. Former Georgia Governor John Clark, his wife Nancy, and 2 grandchildren had all died in 1832 and were buried nearby. The Clarks' home had been located just in front of the West home.

The party enjoyed one more outing on the *Gladys* to Harrison on a moonlit evening before George departed for Chicago on February 2nd. He arrived back in Escanaba to temperatures 16 degrees below zero. He built fires in the house and got the temperature to 14 above zero in the sitting room and 22 degrees in his library. The deep freeze continued until February 28th when the temperature finally rose to 34. But the warm up was short lived and the temperatures dipped below zero until March 16th. George noted in his diary that the roads were ruined. When visiting friends in Escanaba he continuously promoted St. Andrews, its weather, and the opportunities there.

March 25th …Heard clock strike every hour from 2 AM. Feel about same – a dull day. Feel a little better this evening. Have a talk with Garland and Holmes on Florida.

At work he had to write a new time card for the peak season train schedule and add on an extra freight train and passenger train. May 5th he slept a long time in the evening and was *"startled awake by being called – a dream"*. He worked on the railroad, in his garden, and fixed up shelves in the wine cellar until his new "wheel" arrived. He had purchased a bicycle, but did not like the drop handle and "rat trap pedals" so he had to order some new handles and make modifications. He added a cyclometer, rebuilt the handle bars and pedals and then took off riding his wheel. He found the back tire used up quickly and had to order a new one from Chicago. Dell, Nellie and the children returned from St. Andrews at the end of June.

George rode his wheel, went to a bicycle meet, sailed some evenings, and gardened, and walked in the garden. He documented his total miles wheeling at 472 miles during 1895. As August 24th came, the date of his father's death in 1886, George wrote in his diary that he was *"saddened beyond all account"* and *"Wish I were dead"*. Several days later he began to come out of this depression.

In September George started making plans for a kitchen addition at the bay house. It was decided to try California for Dell's health so she went in October and spent a couple of months there. There was little benefit to her. She returned mid-December and the family started preparing to head south to St. Andrews. George took Philip around Chicago with him "trading" and the outing delighted his 7 year old grandson. The family arrived in St. Andrews on Christmas day.

December 25th Up early – got some holly. Get away from Bay Head at 8 (AM) – Pleasant forenoon – Some cloudy – See turkies – Reach home 11:40 (AM) – Found everything all right – Got things all unpacked this PM from trunk and boxes and barrel – All in good shape – Got tree ready and have it at 7:15 PM. Aunt, Uncle and Will Look here. To bed tired out by 10 – I have 3 ties – bookmark from Annie …2 handkerchiefs – suspenders - pocket case.

As usual there was unpacking to do, cleaning up around the house and yard, and George called around to friends in St. Andrews and at Ware Mercantile and Brackin's.

December 31st Clear – working at kitchen painting & c – Lots to do. Have sore throat – Thus ends 95 – A year of many disappointments and lots of work in the last half – Have grown tired of fighting for an existence but it is fight or not exist. What will 96 bring?

1896

The first days of 1896 in St. Andrews were very busy. George hired a man to build the chimney, he made an offer on the lots adjacent to his property on the west side, got lumber for the kitchen addition, got a stove in, and worked around the yard trimming trees, making trellises, tying up honeysuckle, Cherokee Rose, and grape vines, and entertaining visitors who called. In mid-January Dell took a fall coming down the stairs of the house and turned her ankle over. George made crutches for her to use while she recovered.

The *Gladys* needed repairs and the wind blew fiercely for several days, so it was late January before the party was able to take an outing to Land's End for shell collecting and hunting. Will Look, Mr. Holmes and Garland, Mrs. Rolph, Laura, and baby were on the outing. Nellie and the children went along and gathered a great amount of shells. Dell spent the day home alone.

George left the bay by boat at 2:23 AM on January 27th with Capt. Ware. They reached Bay Head at 5:23 AM and from there George took a rig to Chipley, arriving at 4:00 PM to meet the train. He arrived home on January 29th *"once more to work for a long busy year"*.

Dell, Nellie, and the children remained in St. Andrews. Dell's ankle took several weeks to heal, and she was often ill. There were many callers to check on the family. Margery Sheppard and Mrs. Rolph called frequently on Dell. Nellie was often invited to parties at the homes of Mrs. Maxon, Mrs. Gwaltney, and socials at Ware's Hall. Nellie and Grace would go downtown almost each day and on Sundays they went to church.

In April George sent $200.00 to Mr. McKinnie for purchase of the 2 lots west of George's property and the platted street (Fountain Avenue). He routinely sent money to Dell and to Nellie. On an outing to Brandon in May George was disappointed to find the cemetery in bad shape. The graves of West family members were sunken.

Dell was sick periodically during the summer in St. Andrews and she, Nellie, and the children did not return to Escanaba until mid-August. It is often written of Dell being a fragile and ill little woman, which she was, but she also was a capable woman. June 17th she wrote in her diary "*Ran the Gladys for the first time all alone*". Dell also wrote when she had bad days of feeling ill. George worked on the railroad, rode his bicycle, and worked in his garden. In 1896 George rode a total of 750 miles on his wheel. He also spent time with Philip.

August 28th 64 degrees, clear – calm early but a brisk south wind soon began to blow – Philip and I up and out at 6 fishing for perch off the lighthouse point. He catches 2 and I catch 4 – wind came up and drove us in….

George's first entrepreneurial activity in St. Andrews was as a voting stockholder in the St. Andrews Bay, Chipley, and Vernon Telephone Company.

ST. ANDREWS BAY AND CHIPLEY TELE-PHONE COMPANY.

St. Andrews Bay Fla., Sept. 1, 1896.

Mr. G. M. West

Escanaba, Mich.

Dear Sir: There will be a meeting of the stock subscribers to the St. Andrews Bay and Chipley Telephone Company, for the purpose of electing permanent officers and such other business as may come before the meeting, at Ware's Hall, in St. Andrews Bay, on Thursday, Sept. 3, 1896, at 8 o'clock, p. m., at which your attendance is solicited.

As a subscriber to the stock of said Company you will be entitled to 7 1/2 votes in this meeting.

Wm. A. Emmons,

Temporary President,

Attest:

J. R. Hamilton, Temp. Sec'y.

From the Panama City Publishing Company Museum, West Documents Collection

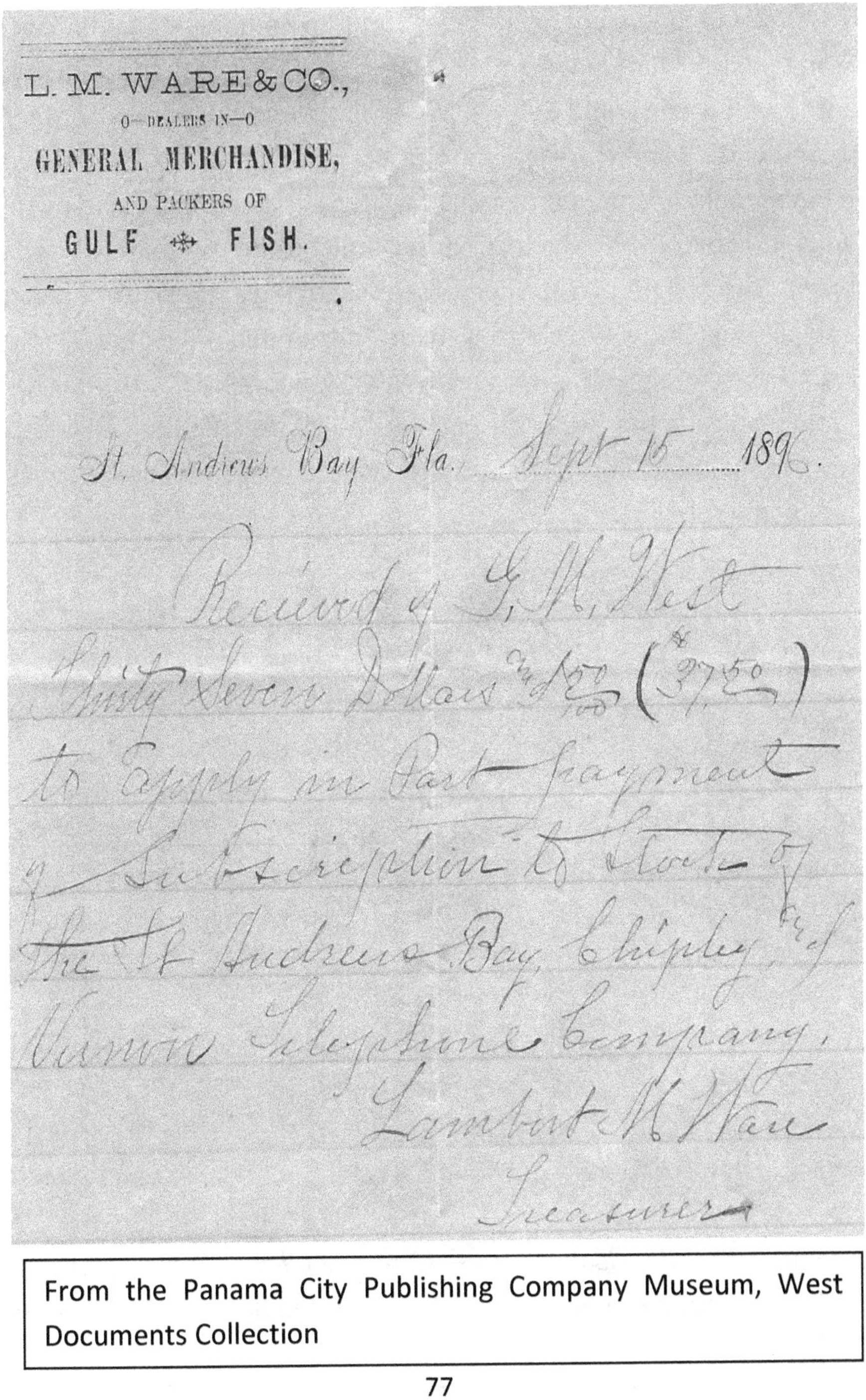

L. M. WARE & CO.,

O—DEALERS IN—O

GENERAL MERCHANDISE,

AND PACKERS OF

GULF ✦ FISH.

St. Andrews Bay Fla. Sept 15 189*6*.

Received of G. M. West
Thirty Seven Dollars & *No/100* ($37.50)
to apply in Part payment
of Subscription to Stock of
the St Andrews Bay, Chipley &
Vernon Telephone Company.

Lambert M Ware

Treasurer

From the Panama City Publishing Company Museum, West
Documents Collection

By November Dell's doctor urged George to send her south at once. Arrangements were made and in a few days Dell went to Birmingham to stay with friends until George, Nellie, and the children met her there December 22nd and travelled on together to St. Andrews. They arrived on December 24th, had a nice cedar tree for Christmas and an enjoyable evening, though they were tired and cold from the journey. Many friends called on them over the next couple of days and all were feeling good except Grace who was ill with "distemper". George worked around the house and yard, and was very impressed with one rose bloom he picked that was 2 ½" high by 4 ½" across. He hung a swing in the yard for the children, went up to Ware's for some naptha for the boat, and wrote letters.

Philip and Grace West, GMW Collection, BCPL

December 31st 64, clear all day – 72 nearly all the time – I feel some tired all day but more rested at night – Trim the Burbank plum today –

also clear around the shop outside – stake trees & c (such). Henry at the front yard – Put up some pictures this PM. A SE wind all day but quiet tonight. Very high tide this evening as I go after the mail – About 8 more come tonight – it not reaching Bay Head in time to come on. Children better today – Quiet this evening as I write this last record for 1896. What has 1897 in store for me?

1897

January 1ˢᵗ 66 degrees, a clear day – SE wind – Been warm all night – wind grows with the day. I get at the pictures today – put them all up – Dell taken sick at noon. Distemper aggravated her back trouble terrible pain. Got some morphine and inject it – first time I ever done so – Frank took Grace and boys to Cromanton today in launch. A busy day with me. To PO at night – a high tide. Picked some nice roses.....

January 5ᵗʰ 42 degrees, NW wind, clear – Mr. Singletary came this AM. At walk today after fixing lock to door – Dockstader at pond hole and helping on walk – I keep busy at everything. Box from home in on boat this AM and box trees – got them down this PM. Opened box from house and got things all fixed up – Dell about same – Busy day. Venus and the new moon very beautiful tonight.

January 6ᵗʰ 36 degrees, Clear, NW wind – a white frost this AM. Dockstader and I put out trees. Singletary at the walk – Henry and Alex Register with cart at hauling. Get a good days work done – 50 trees out – walk done and good. Got stuff hauled on to lot for trees – a busy day in every way. Italians with hand organ around this AM. Clear and cool tonight – 37 degrees at 6 PM.

Mr. Dockstader George mentioned was handy and did a lot of work for George around the yard and house. Dell was in poor condition, the weather continued to be cold with occasional windy days, so George and the men he had hired to help him stayed busy on the yard and house. There was plenty to do there as more and more trees and plants arrived for the yard.

In mid-January George had lumber ordered and was building a grape arbor and a playhouse for the children. He and 3 men, Richard, Dockstader, and Henry, did an incredible amount of work on the property. They did trimming, clearing, repairs, building, digging around the pond and fixing a border for it, and working on smoothing the road to George's house. Once the pond was completed George drew it on the map he was making of his property.

George finished building the playhouse for the children and put together a lantern show to entertain friends and neighbors. Attendance at the show included Aunt Sarah, the Mitchells, Maxons, Greens, Capt. Ware, Mr. Hilton, Mrs. Pierce and Mrs. Bennett. George took some of them home in the launch at midnight. The next evening Nellie had a party of young people over and George presented the lantern show again. These shows could have been pictures George had taken and also some slides he ordered that were views of sights from around the world. The next evening George was able to go fire fishing at the lagoon. His catch included a 10 pound redfish 30 inches long. He baked it for dinner.

The weather warmed enough and the wind calmed down enough for Dell, Philip, Aunt Sarah, and George to take a trip to Lands End and Hurricane Island for shell collecting. George also gathered pitcher plants to take home and put in his yard.

Unidentified people on the beach,

GMW Collection, BCPL

The mail delivery had become so unreliable George talked about the route with Capt. Ware before leaving for Chicago. He set off at 2:30 AM from Ware's dock on January 27th in a cold wind and rain. The small party made it to Bay Head by boat at 6:40 AM and to Chipley in rigs by 6:00 PM where they caught the train. Dell remained in St. Andrews and George sent her a message over the phone and wrote to her from each stop. He arrived home on January 30th feeling as though he had only been away a day or two and he weighed 179 pounds, 6 less than when he went south.

The first task after clearing away his desk was to get up a bond and submit a bid for the mail route in St. Andrews. George was keen on promptness and the mail delivery in St. Andrews had been frequently late and unreliable. There was never indication he was awarded the route.

In May he ordered a new boat. He took 100 tulip bulbs and visited the cemetery in Brandon where he planted those. Letters from Nellie and Dell brought the news that Dell had been "sick abed" for some time. This delayed them travelling back to Escanaba. George spent an afternoon at the race track watching the horses. He also kept busy getting his garden planted with peas, lettuce, and beans. It was nice enough weather to start riding his wheel again, particularly at night on a full moon.

On July 7th Dell, Nellie and children returned to Escanaba. Immediately upon return, Nellie and the children moved out of the West home where they had been since Charles' death in 1892. George was very blue over it and shocked. He and Dell still saw the children and Nellie often for dinner, picnics, concerts, the circus, and for George and Philip to ride bicycles. At the Escanaba house George had sewer lines installed.

November 2nd was a dark day as Dr. Booth reported Nellie's sample had bacilli in it. The bacilli George refers to could mean she had what was called "consumption" in the 1800's, known to us as tuberculosis, possibly the same disease that took Charles. The bacteria was commonly contracted from contaminated milk and most often attacked the lungs, but also other organs. A person could carry the bacteria for some time before symptoms of weight loss, chest pain, and weakness appeared.

Nellie talked with her folks and George about herself. She wanted to go to New Mexico, possibly in hopes of the climate helping her condition. She never went to New Mexico, but instead went to St.

Andrews with Dell and the children on December 12th. George joined them in time to have the Christmas tree on December 24th as was customary. Several friends joined them at the tree including the Knowles family.

There was a lot of trimming and cleaning up to do around the house and property, and his launch *Gladys* was in bad shape.

December 31st 66 degrees, Part cloudy – SW gale on – moist – rained a little at 10 PM when the wind went in to the NW. Began to grow cooler. 36 degrees at 9 PM and blew heavily from the NW at 6 PM til 12 (midnight) – Burned and cleared and trimmed trees and rose bushes. The old year gives out with a terrible NW gale – a very disappointing ending to a perplexing year. Cleaned out cupboards today. Have following nice fruit – 12 qt pears, 49 qts pickled pears, 13 qts figs, 8 qts blackberries, 8 qts mulberries, 11 qts jelly – mostly plum.

1898

George's 1898 diary gives a glimpse of his physical build at the time. In the front of the diary is a page to record sizes and his were: weight: 184, hat: 7 ¼, gloves: 8, hosiery: 10 ½, collar: 16, cuffs: 8, shoes: 8.

The first few days of January in St. Andrews were wet with the temperatures of 20 degrees and the NW wind blew a gale. The ice was layered 2 inches thick everywhere. It did not take long though and the temperatures rose to 70 degrees in the day and 50 degrees at night. George was able to get the *Gladys* repaired and start venturing out on the water. He also resumed his work around the property. In the house during the evening he started his work on the West genealogical tables.

One of his favorite hobbies had always been making flower arrangements and bouquets. He picked a bowl of hyacinths and fixed palmetto and yaupon for table decorations. Outside he started bamboo, hibiscus, oleanders, tea plant, olive, blue water lily, blue water hyacinth, 2 altheas, 1 cedar, and he put a box around the plant in front. While uptown by boat the family took turns on the scale. Nellie weighed 124 pounds, and 6-year-old Grace 49 pounds. The temperatures were near 70 and they "took" ice cream almost daily.

January 26th George started for Escanaba. He arrived there to below zero temperatures and the railroad extremely busy from the weather, wrecks, and legal issues. Pain in his chest and right arm were relentless and on February 24th he was "lifeless", but just 2 days later he was feeling alive and ambitious. Dell and Nellie wrote him frequently and George wrote to them often. He faithfully sent money to Nellie and Dell each pay day. Dell wrote of them going camping at St. Joe in early March.

In the weeks leading up to the April ice thaw and the docks opening up, George was very ill with a severe cold in his throat, nose, and head. But there was the new card to make up for the train schedules, there were train wrecks and injuries including 2 men losing a leg each, and ultimately neither man surviving, and Dell remained in St. Andrews "sick abed". Though he was depressed and blue many days he ordered a new wheel and began riding often and for long distances. With the daytime temperatures staying above freezing, George also began to prepare his garden and plant seeds.

The family returned to Escanaba on June 16th and George bought Philip a new wheel. The Lemen Circus was in Escanaba on July 13th and family attended as did about 800 people.

On July 31st Escanaba experienced the worst fire in its history. George and the other men worked at extinguishing the fire well into the night, but almost the entire block and some other buildings around it burned. It started in Fogarty's Flour and Feed store and raged out of control. The dry goods store, Soo Line ticket office, Western Express, jewelry store, tea store, clothing store, and bakery were all destroyed. The Escanaba Bank, Catholic Church, school, drug store, the electric light lines, and several other buildings nearby also burned. The losses not covered by insurance exceeded $200,000. The St. Paul Globe printed an account on the August 1st, 1898 front page.

George visited his friend Frank and took a basket of bottles to him. Frank filled the bottles with his whiskey and returned those to George.

On August 20th George addressed the Union meeting of train men at the hall. It was a successful affair and George received this letter afterwards:

"Dear Sir, in behalf of the different RR organizations...I take pleasure in thanking you for the many courtesies extended to us and your most generous cooperation in aiding us. Therefore making our union meeting a Grand Success and I also wish to congratulate you on your most able and eloquent address. I have heard nothing but words of praise in regard to same since meeting...

Respect, E. E. Wood, Secretary, Joint Committee"

Nellie's condition worsened, she felt poorly often, and in September began to spend more days in bed. By November she was bedridden at her mother's home. To Nellie's pleasure, George visited every day and he and Dell had the children most of the time. On the 23rd she discussed her affairs with George and appointed him executor and guardian of Philip, about to turn 10 years old, and 7-year-old Grace. At home George sorted the remainder of Charles' letters and papers and burned them.

December 8th Clear and cloudy – a cold raw day – NW wind. Over to Nellie's at 12 midnight last night. She was so comfortable – much weaker this noon. Was called at 5:20 as she was failing fast – Staid with her until the end which came at 9:20 PM. Peacefully at last – Poor girlie...

December 11th A very busy day. Up early and to office. At 9 go to cemetery and take up baby – Nothing left... Over to Nellie's and fix flowers Funeral services at 3 – Drawn in sleigh – Get ready to go to Brandon with coach on 2 – all off safely on time...

"Take up baby" could be referring to Philip's twin Ernest born in 1888. That infant was buried in Escanaba initially and they planned to move the remains to the family plot in Brandon Cemetery.

December 12th Lay at Fond Du Lac until 7:30 AM. Special to Burnett Junction – St. Paul from there to Brandon on time – Set coach on siding. I go to cemetery and see that all is ok. Met Ella south at Waupun. Services at 11:15 – very cold and high north wind – To Edith's for dinner. Took children out in PM. Start back at 4:40...

About Nellie's death Aunt Sarah wrote to George *"...If Nellie must go, we ought to be glad her suffering is at an end, but it is hard to part with our loved ones and Nellie was with me so much during Hinez's sickness that I feel her loss very keenly, it seems to bring his death back so forcibly....I wish I could go with you to lay her away..."*

The family had their Christmas tree in Escanaba with the children on December 24th and then on the 27th headed south for St. Andrews. On the train trip through Alabama George noted that there was a lot of cotton still in the fields and many were out picking. The Wests arrived by train in Chipley on December 31st.

December 31st Commenced raining hard about 2 AM. Rained or poured until noon – Frank arrived with (the) Gladys about 11 – I get some yellow and red holly. After dinner conclude to start – get away at 2 PM. No rain this PM. Found place looking best it has in years. Lots of Roman Hyacinths and narcissus but few roses – supper at 6 – arrived at 5. Up town and get some provisions – feel well – Thus ends 1898. Sorrow – some joys – and much very hard work. The hardest fall I ever had here in the work.

1899

George spent days in the regular routine of cleaning, clearing, building the walks, and getting settled in the house. He also begin the task of cleaning and clearing on the acquired lots to the east of his house, and making a place in the hen yard for 2 guineas he bought. He also purchased for 50 cents a Minorca rooster from the Surber family and he rented Bert Ware's bicycle for $1 a week.

January 21st and they were able to take a trip in the *Gladys*, starting up East Bay at 10:00 AM. George took a picture at Bunkers Cove, then went on to Parker, Pittsburg, and to Col. Walkley's where he bought 2 roosters, a Golden Wyandotte and a Brown leghorn. They were home at 5:00 PM.

The next day they went to the sand hills on the Gulf gathering shells and taking pictures. He and Philip went hunting at the Lagoon, bagged a turkey and 2 ducks. George departed for Escanaba on the 26th and when he boarded the train wrote in his diary *"On the cars once again for a long season of hard work at home."*

The train trip home was wrought with trouble. The train he was to board was 2 hours late, then while underway the train broke apart 3 times and George arrived in Escanaba to temperatures 25 degrees below zero, 75 degrees colder than in Florida. This was the worst winter on the railroad George had seen. In February the temperature rarely got above zero. Trains had problems up and down the rails and frequently the wrecking car was sent in, but not before a crew, many times including George, would clear the tracks of snow drifts. Even by April there was still 2 feet of snow and ice everywhere, and not a bare spot to be seen.

When spring did come George rode his new wheel, wrote letters to Grace and Philip, and Dell wrote to George that she did not want to return to Escanaba. They did return on July 1st. George was attentive to providing the children opportunities. In particular they were provided music lessons. Grace played piano and Philip the saxophone.

George battled a severe cold the rest of the summer. He went to the office but could hardly get back home for the suffocating feeling and weakness. His taste was gone, he had an awful cough, and he tried all the remedies he knew: hot bath, alcohol in his throat, phosphates, liniment on his throat, but to no avail. Then Grace was ill most of August with a cough and fever. Dell was also ill the entire month. There was so much sickness, but no let up in the work. By mid-September Dell was pushing to return to St. Andrews, but the illnesses kept everyone in Escanaba. Frank and Lizzie Lathrup were close friends of George and Dell. They travelled to St. Andrews often, and Frank also spent time with Philip. Frank had appendicitis and had to have an operation and was hospitalized for most of the month. The railroad was extremely busy, but 20 men were out of work sick. October 13th Philip came home from school sick with the cold and fever.

Finally, on December 18th Dell and the children left for St. Andrews. They stopped in Birmingham with friends to wait for George who joined them on the 23rd. They had their Christmas tree in Birmingham. George received a tie, napkin ring marker, initial plate, cup, mug, perfume, atomizer, match receiver, and dishes. Always interested in business, he went out to see the new steel plant at Ensley, Alabama.

They took the train on to Pensacola and Chipley, then had an eventful trip from there. George was driving the rig with his party, and a second rig had the trunks and supplies.

December 27th In Pensacola on time – part cloudy – Out at 7 – awful hot in sleeper all night. 25 minutes late in to Chipley. Got out at 11:40. I drive one rig. 2 boys on the other. Get along well until 10 miles out. Boys have a jug whiskey and are getting drunk – one fell off – like to run over him. Jug fell off. I ran over it try to break it, can't. Other boy has a revolver and is firing it promiscuously – decide to go ahead and get folks through – dark and misty at time – Get off road below Sulphur springs – lost 20 minutes – got back and in Bay Head 10:15 – Boys show up 11:20 – Get off 11:40 - Dave met us with boat.

The party arrived in St. Andrews at 2:20 in the morning, and slept in until 8:00 AM. George got to work on unpacking, fixing up things, and making butter.

December 31st 40 degrees this AM at 9 – 32 degrees in the night. Wind east – cold and rain. Goes to the north and rains. Fix up all curtains and pictures. Quiet day. Feeling little better. 2 quarts milk this AM. A quart and a half tonight. 6 eggs – Thus ends 1899. A busy year – and successful in many ways. I have grown older and failed in health some – The children are disappointing in some ways – Philip especially – and he has worried me. What will the 1900's bring me –

1900

January 3rd 22 degrees above this morning and the wind still north west. Clear – Everything frozen solid. Ice in the kitchen. The Old Town bayou (now Lake Caroline) was covered with ice this PM. Never saw it so before. Got up to 43 degrees today – but wind is still northwest....

January 7th 46 degrees last night – 56 when get up. 68-70 during the day – Cleaned up the dark room – fixed pictures all over the house. Feeling more like myself today than have in a long time. ...A beautiful day. Looked over Aunt Sarah's house this evening. On owls Agnes says Naomi says to her when she hears an owl hooting at night "Turn your pockets (inside out) which surely scares them away". A sure way to get short of them.

Philip, now 11 years old, attended school while in St. Andrews. George set to work on the property, got more lumber to build a wood shed, finish the veranda on the front of the house, and a pig pen. He hired Wiley and they used Hawk's boat, *Jerome L. Rogers,* to haul 1,000 feet of lumber. They also built a bench and fixed the stairs to the beach in front. At night they had a bonfire and roasted oysters they harvested from Ware's point. The family went over to the lagoon and Spanish Shanty Cove. They collected shells on the beach, and George rode his rented bicycle on the beach. Oysters and conchs were gathered and roasted on the beach.

On the 22nd George was off to Escanaba at 4:30 AM on a bright moonlit night. Dell rode along in the boat to Bay Head and returned to St. Andrews after George disembarked at 7:40 AM. The rig was there to meet him and he travelled a new road from Gainers to White Oak, then Chipley. The train trip was not so quiet this time.

January 24th About 3 AM was awakened by a crash on my side of car. Train southbound on siding had run into sleeper I was in at my feet – through crossover switch which was wrong. Broke in side of sleeper from berth 9 to vestibule and broke that on the head and rear car. No one hurt – In Chicago 20 minutes late.

Upon his return to work George learned of conversations taking place among his superiors. One wanted to bring in a replacement for George and the other was defending George. The issue was temporarily set aside when a warehouse fire at the docks and also a deadly train crash distracted them. The next few days are best told in George's on words:

February 8th Raining when we get to Powers little after midnight – See flames in sky Escanaba ward just before reach Powers. Message there tells of fire at USWW plant since 11:45. Hurry in – little after 1 when we get there. Fire still very hot – some buildings not yet afire – barn & c. Dock approach wet down – Pump house is on fire and Mr. Slater and I at that. Got wet and cold. Home after 3....Just as am getting up from supper phoned that (engine) 289 was in to (engine) 21 at Ford River – Many killed and injured and wreck on fire....Called Drs and started in less than 15 minutes – There at 7:20 collision occurred 6:35. Got pails – done all could to put out fire. Used up all water – got wounded – 11 PM arrange to go back at day light for bodies – working at office at midnight.

February 9th To bed less than 2 hours when Mr. Ashton wished me at office to talk over accident. Was at office until after 4 AM. Laid down on lounge at home but could not get to sleep – cold – 5 below this morning....Had time with freezing water on clothing – was wet and then scorched. Out at 7:20 AM with Oliner undertaker. Picked up remains 9 people. Done all work myself that I might identify them. But little left in wreck of anyone – 5 passengers injured. Warner Brown one of them. 8 killed and 7 of them burned and 2 trainmen killed are burned ... I get in 1 PM. Busy afternoon – To bed 8 PM 63 hours with less than 3 hours sleep.

February 13th ...the inquest is held today – Began at 10 AM at Court House. ...Inquest over at 4 PM. I was on stand – verdict – cause accident snow storm and smoke from the kilns.

February 15th 10 below zero – been 13 – clear. All day taking evidence - ...I rush all day long. Kept 3 stenographers busy. Am feeling strong this afternoon. Very tired tonight – Send in result my investigation...

From the Racine Daily Journal Wisconsin:

Escanaba, Mich., Feb. 9, 1900. -- By all odds the most disastrous wreck ever known on the Peninsula division of the Chicago & Northwestern railway occurred late Thursday night at Ford River switch, seven miles south of here. Nine people were killed and six were injured, two fatally. The accident was caused by the fast freight, No. 289 crashing into the rear of the Felch branch accommodation. The accommodation train was late, and had stopped at Ford River switch to take on some passengers. From the facts reported it encroached on the freight's time. Just as the accommodation was ready to pull out the freight train came tearing along at the rate of a mile a minute on a straight track and in a blinding snowstorm. The train instantly caught fire, and four bodies, beyond the power of the rescuing party to save, were burned. A rescuing party, including every doctor in this city, was hastily sent to the scene, and all injured and dead have been brought here.

After the tumultuous days, changes were made in positions at Escanaba. George remained Assistant Superintendent, but C. E. Andrews was brought in as Train Master. George's office was moved into a cold, barn-like adjacent room, and he viewed this as an attempt to crowd him out.

The next couple of nights George recorded his dreams that had bewildered him. At 4:00 in the morning he awoke, thinking he took a penny off his hip and laid it in the bed. In the morning he could not find it and concluded it was a dream. The next night he awoke at 12:20, lying on his right side as the night before, and felt something near his hand again. He took hold of it and it was a penny. He got up and made sure of it, and laid it on the dresser. It was a puzzle to him, as "Mrs. M" had made up the bed the day before, turned it all over, and nothing was there. George wondered where it had come from. Folklore of the day was that a penny that appears is a sign of your guardian angel coming by.

In the spring George shipped Philip's wheel to him at the bay so he could ride there. Grace wrote to George and asked to stay in St. Andrews for the summer.

Railroad officials from Chicago came to Escanaba, met with George and toured the area. George believed they were assessing the value of the men working there. Cold weather continued into the spring and there were derailments and several accidents and deaths on the railroad. A new turn table was installed at the roundhouse in the Escanaba rail yard.

Early in June George submitted a package of his photographs to Ladies Home Journal. No letters from Dell came, but Philip and Grace wrote to George that Dell was "sick abed". She finally wrote to George at the end of June and was no better. George packed a trunk and headed to St. Andrews on July 2nd. On the train ride south going through Alabama he noted that the cotton looked poorly. He arrived July 4th and found Dell in poor condition. He spent time with the children "bathing" in the bay at noon time, and then he went in the bay in the evenings to cool off from the hot July days. After several days, Dell managed to join the family at the table for dinner. With her in better condition George made plans to return to Escanaba.

July 16th Leave home at 1 AM. Nice night – bright moonlight – Pick up Capt. Ware. 2 hours 30 minutes in to Bay Head. Frank ran boat – not ready to start. Get off 5:20. Warm day – very sleepy. Pleasant country. Showers from Orange Hill in. 4.00 for trip. Got trunk checked. Off 30 minutes late. Lots peaches being shipped from here.

He arrived back in Escanaba to more turnovers in the railroad positions and in August word of Dell's new ailments came to him. She had a lump on her breast and the doctor feared it was cancer. George was distraught worrying what was next.

September 11th ...Storm gets here by noon over an inch and a half rain fell this PM. Wind went to north at 1 PM and blows a gale all PM and in tonight. Our share of the Gulf hurricane.

On September 8, 1900, a Category 4 hurricane ripped through Galveston, Texas, killing an estimated 6,000 to 8,000 people, and an upwards total of 12,000 after it moved across the mid-west and New England states. At the time of the 1900 hurricane, Galveston, nicknamed the Oleander City, was filled with vacationers.

Sophisticated weather forecasting technology didn't exist at the time, but the U.S. Weather Bureau issued warnings telling people to move to higher ground. However, these advisories were ignored by many vacationers and residents alike. A 15-foot storm surge flooded the city, which was then situated at less than 9 feet above sea level, and numerous homes and buildings were destroyed. The remnants of the storm blew through Escanaba.

In October George was inspired to enter the banking industry and talked with several associates about the opportunity. He knew his position at work was insecure and he was looking to new possibilities. W. B. Linsley, his long time friend and superior at work, requested George let C. E. Andrews work on the winter time card for the trains and George teach him how it was done. The new time card had to be out by November 25th, and it was, with 4 errors. George wrote "*I do not work like that*".

He had turkey dinner alone on Thanksgiving, November 29th, but enjoyed the quiet day. Then December 5th came the news he had expected. "*Mr. L* (Linsley) *came in and advised me that the Company were to be through with my services January 1st. A shock of course – though I have had so many things this year indicate such was to be my fate that I ought not to be surprised...*"

The release brought some relief and George moved his desk and papers from his railroad office to his home. December 19th he was able to travel back to St. Andrews. He took a boat from Pensacola and they dropped anchor sometime after 9:00 PM on December 21st just off Land's End to wait for daylight to find the East Pass. At midnight the wind shifted and the waves made the boat pitch and lunge. George woke 3 boys and they moved the boat away from the shore to smoother water. At daylight they saw the waves breaking all across the West Pass and they ran the boat to the East Pass in a heavy southeast sea and into St. Andrews Bay. He arrived home at 8:05 AM and found everything to be as usual.

Christmas Eve George got a tree set up and the family and some friends had Christmas with lots of presents. On the 26th George had a phone installed at the house. It took from 7:30 in the morning until 2:00 PM and when connected it worked well.

George wrote that on December 27th Frank got a big sawfish at Wares Point as he comes home in the boat. The sawfish is of the ray family, found in tropical and sub-tropical waters, and estuaries. Once a common sighting in St. Andrews Bay, to date the last sawfish sighted in Northwest Florida was in the 1940's. They are a protected species.

December 31st ...Thus ends the most memorable year of my life – I am tired out with its worries – and it has brought me but little else. But I trust that I can take up something the coming year that will not exhaust me as the work has lately which I now lay down.

1901

The first few days of January were rainy and limited what George could do. He did kill one of the pigs, weighing in at 160 pounds, and he collected the lard, salted the pork, gave some to friends and sold some. He wrote letters to railroad associates to find out if there was any change in his employment situation. It must have been very disturbing to him to be unemployed at 55 years old, having worked since he was 15 years old. The rain finally subsided and he was able to clean out his pigeon and hen coops. He put carpet on the stairs in the house. The next days were beautiful, with stunning sunsets, and trips to Hurricane

Island to gather shells. He worked in the yard and garden, putting out cabbage plants and beets, and hoeing around the carrots.

January 26th George headed back to Escanaba. He worked at his desk at home writing letters, working on Nellie's estate affairs, and promoting a bank project to potential partners but with no success. He did manage to sell some lots he owned in Escanaba and on March 11th decided to go back to St. Andrews. He caught the mail boat at Bay Head and arrived home at 7:50 PM on March 14th.

It was a cold and windy spell of weather in St. Andrews. George spent time with Dr. Booth going over to Harrison, Smack Bayou, and to look at property near Pretty Bayou. He received a letter from Mr. Kilgallen offering him a Superintendent position at Chicago Terminal Transfer Railroad. April 5th he set off for Escanaba. Philip rode with him as far as Birmingham. George admired the rhododendrons in bloom in Florida, and the peach trees and redbuds dotted the landscape in Alabama.

George arrived at his house in Escanaba on April 8th, gathered what he would need and left that evening for Chicago. He wrote *"So I leave Escanaba"*. He met with Kilgallen several times the next few days and began work there out of *"a barn for an office"*. He ordered a Smith Premier typewriter, met up with William J. Jackson, who became a close friend, and he resided temporarily at Briggs House Hotel.

William J. Jackson, signed "to my good friend West", GMW Collection, BCPL

The Chicago Terminal Transfer Railroad Company (CTT) had tracks in Chicago that provided connection for the several railroad companies that came through or terminated at Chicago. The CTT gave the various other railroad companies access to Grand Central Station in Chicago and it also served to connect those railroads for freight transfers. George's job included coordination with other railroads and the arrangement for usage of the tracks, and provide crossings over other rail line tracks as he did for the Elgin Joliet & Eastern Railroad and the Inland North West Railroad. He also measured the grade of tracks, calculated the speed at which a train could pass through, and planned the most efficient, safe, and cost-effective operations on the tracks.

He was responsible for all operations being in compliance with government regulations and union agreements. Additionally, he was responsible for maintaining a good relationship with the workers and the customers. There were factories and industry on this south side of Chicago and there were many spurs off the track to service each. One was Aermotor Windmill Company. There windmills were made for pumping water from the ground, and fire towers were made also. In 2019 there were over 2 dozen Aermotor windmills from New York to California on the National Register of Historic Places.

The coming and going of freight trains had to be coordinated and billed along with the through traffic and those going to Grand Central Station. George was perfect for the job. He was keen on being precise with time and budgets. He was thorough at completing his weekly reports about the yard activity.

Things started out rough and difficult at this job. When George's superior came down and gave the men a "roasting" for alleged offenses George could not stand it. He went to Mr. Kilgallen and after a talk was put at ease. A month later the same occurred.

May 29ᵗʰ ....Message this forenoon by phone that Superintendents would be here this PM. Came at 1:40 . Rawhided every thing up and down – Took them out around town. Went away at 6:25. I feel very much upset.

May 30ᵗʰ ....In town 7:24 Met Mr. Kilgallen. Talked with him til 1:30...I feel better after talking with him...

Dell had been ill much of the spring. Ella wrote George that she, Dell, and the children would be leaving from St. Andrews on Sunday evening, June 16ᵗʰ, and would wire him from Pensacola. The letter came to George on Wednesday the 19ᵗʰ and there had been no word from the party. Friday he finally received word. The group had taken a boat from St. Andrews to Pensacola and had been caught out in a gale in the Gulf. The boat returned to port and the group took the inland route to Chipley, and then by train to Pensacola. All were safe in Pensacola and would tarry in Birmingham before coming on north. They arrived in Chicago June 30ᵗʰ.

George reserved 2 additional rooms at the hotel for the family. Dell rested and he took the children to Lincoln Park for the afternoon to stay cool. July 4ᵗʰ they took Chicago's elevated train, known as the "L", to Sheridan Park. He accompanied the family to Escanaba on July 6ᵗʰ, and returned to work in Chicago once he had them settled.

In his unending curiosity about the world, and thirst for knowledge, George bought the latest book, *The Sea Beach at Ebb Tide*. Written by Augusta Foote Arnold and published in 1901 the book was a guide to seaweed and lower animal life found between tidemarks. George also spent many evenings in the public library in Chicago. On July 17th he attended the Buffalo Bill show. He went to the Masonic Temple Roof Garden on July 20th with a friend, Mr. Hook. The building was the tallest in Chicago from 1895 to 1920, having 21 stories, 302 feet tall, and a garden on the top with a glass roof. He attended the play *Under Two Flags* and wrote in his diary that he did not like it.

On September 13th news broke that President McKinley would not survive the gun wounds of his attempted assassination. At 2:15 AM in the night he died and Theodore Roosevelt was sworn into office.

September 15th Cloudy dismal day. Dell very very nervous. Have Dr. B over – and he thinks she must go south. I do not know what to do. She wants to pack up things here and take many south. Go back (to Chicago) at 9 – all used up every way. I can not stand this trouble as I used to.

Then by September 20th Dell had almost everything packed up. She and the children joined George in Chicago. He took the children (now 12 and 10 years old) to the Public library and park, and to see one of the most popular plays of the time, "Way Down East". Penned by Charlotte Blair Parker in 1897, performed steadily for 2 decades, the sentimental melodrama is about the travails of a seduced woman, who is cast out by those who learn her story. After being seduced, left, and losing the child from the liaison, she wanders despondently until she finds refuge as a servant in a New England farm. Ignorant of her past, the family embraces her as part of their household. But when the man of the house learns her history he drives her from his home in the midst of a raging snowstorm. She loses her way and nearly dies before she is rescued by the son who loves her and finally persuades his parents that she is worthy to be his wife.

George decided to change accommodations and secured board at the Elliott House for 3.00 per week per child, and 4.50 per week for him and Dell. In his spare time he worked on his booklet about the Hepaticus plant, got those printed, and then he folded them and took them to a binder. Dell and the children went on to St. Andrews on November 12th.

George spent his 56th birthday at home in Escanaba.

November 28th Home 5:36. Cloudy day. Snow on the ground. Rest in house all day. Nice dinner – champaign. Packed up my dictionary & map book...Start back 9 PM. Take Milwaukee sleeper from Powers. Thus ends my birthday.

The new job continued to be quite stressful, to the point George was inclined to quit. The burden he carried about work, Dell's health, and the children was telling upon him. He packed and went to St. Andrews, arriving just after midnight on December 24th. Christmas Eve day he, Philip, and Grace went to find a tree, and brought home a cedar to decorate. The children had a great many presents and all enjoyed the Christmas Eve. Christmas day Hawk came over.

December 31st ...A pretty sunset. Thus ends 1901 – a year of many changes to me and mine – a busy rushing year in a business way – but not much profit in it.

1902

The West family and several friends enjoyed the first day of 1902 on the Gulf beach. They collected 200 oysters and came home at 4:00 to bake the oysters on the beach at the house. The days were chilly but beautiful, and George did some work around the yard, visited friends, went hunting in West Bay, and there was a Masquerade to attend, most likely at Ware's Hall. George stayed home with the children and Dr. Booth.

January 5th George left for Chicago. Work was busy but he managed it smoothly and wrote in his diary *"Do not rush matters and try to take it cool"*. He spent his free time at the library, and writing to Providence and North Scituate in Rhode Island about West family records. George took interest in local politics in Chicago and attended the council meetings.

January 22nd Cloudy – about 26 degrees – Damp. Feel fairly well. Got my NW (Chicago & Northwestern RR) passes today. Do lots writing and some walking. Go in to City at 4:10. Go out to the coliseum. Foggy – misty and unpleasant. After I had been in the building a short time felt very strange – was weak seemingly faint – and perspired fearfully on my face and head. Had to sit down and did not know as could walk to depot. Got over it some soon and went to train. Home on 7 PM. Feel shaky.

George didn't know if he had *"nervous shock, heart failure, or what"*. He felt a little better each day but went to Dr. A. L. Blackwell for an exam. The doctor said his heart was alright except a slight lack of closing of the valve in the upper right chamber. He spent the next several days taking things at a slower pace and resting more. On February 22nd he met with 3 of his superiors at work and wrote *"have a good time and come out in good shape"*.

On March 3rd George was a witness to history as Prince Henry of Prussia toured the US and arrived in Chicago for a parade, receptions, a concert and banquet. The excitement of seeing the royalty pass through the streets of Chicago was quickly overshadowed by a letter from Grace saying Dell was sick. Worry over Dell and work weighed on George's mind constantly.

March 24th ...A nice clear day – I am called in by Kilgallen who is very aggressive and tries to make out I told him and Wacker Saturday that engine 218 was in good order – I told them the 217 was. He is a fool and knave. I am thoroughly disgusted over it all...See Kilgallen at 4. Is as meek as Moses – Boys say had evidently been out last night...

In June, George burned his cheek and chin, but didn't say how. Maybe he did it somehow at work around the steam engines. He got medicine from the doctor and the next day went back and the doctor burned his face with bi-chloride mercury. Commonly used in that era for medicinal purposes, its use was discontinued because of the toxicity of the mercury. Its use in pesticides and wood preservatives continued. George's burns took several weeks to begin healing.

Dell and the children arrived in Chicago on August 2nd. George spent time taking the children to the parks, and to the Field Museum. Still in operation in 2020, this natural history museum originated with a display of artifacts in 1893 at the World's Columbian Exposition. It is named in honor of its first major benefactor, department store magnate Marshall Field. George and the children also attended the stage musical "Sleeping Beauty and the Beast" at the Illinois Theatre.

Ever inquisitive, George went to the Chicago Auditorium and heard John Alexander Dowie speak. Dowie was a self-proclaimed evangelist and faith healer. His "healings" were staged with people planted in the crowd, and his following grew to over 6,000 by 1900. He purchased land 40 miles north of Chicago and founded the town of Zion. He preached humility and self-denial, yet required his followers to deposit their money in his fake bank, the Zion Bank, and he used that to fund his own extravagant lifestyle. After a stroke he went to Mexico to recover and while away his chief lieutenant took control.

In October George went to Escanaba and packed his books and other belongings and made arrangements to sell or rent the house. Later that month Philip had emergency surgery on his throat and nasal passage. He stood it well and recovered quickly. George paid $5.00 for the gas and $35.00 for the services. Less than a week later Dell and the children left for Florida. Philip was doing well, but George wrote in his diary that Dell weighed 96 pounds, and Grace 79, and he felt neither was well. He felt very lonesome after they left.

George kept busy at work, studied business opportunities, and wrote to W. A. Emmons, publisher of the St. Andrews Buoy newspaper. A gentleman named Mr. Gordon called on George and discussed railroad work relative to St. Andrews. There was no track to the St. Andrews Bay area at the time. They met twice, and then began corresponding about raising funds and acquisition of land to build the railroad.

He visited a Chicago shell collector, Mrs. S. A. Williams, and enjoyed seeing her wonderful collection, and sold her one of his Junonia shells for $7.00.

Before he could leave for St. Andrews in December, he received a letter from Dell that Philip had been ill, having a *"rush of blood to his head"*. Despondent, George wrote *"what will come to me next?"* On the 20th he left for St. Andrews, and being a gentleman, gave up his berth on the train to a lady. He arrived in St. Andrews via the mail boat on December 22nd at 7:15 PM.

The family got a Christmas tree from the back of Mr. Gwaltney's property, and decorated it and loaded it with presents for all to enjoy.

George received a new fountain pen (he had lost his a few weeks prior), safety razor, ink stand, hosiery stretcher, stockings, and a tie. After Christmas he had several men at the property helping him clear up the 2 lots to the east that he had just purchased from the Bryans, Block 12, lots 1 & 8. Those are located along the east side of Flower Ave, between Beach Drive and Baker Court.

December 31st ...Boat broke down this AM. Frank launched the (vessel) Laura this evening – Roffman began work 9:30 AM on walk. We fixed up old walks and started on new one today. Baker up to see about fence. I agree to leave street and he says he will look after trespassers in summer time – Philip feeling poorly today. This ends 1902. Warm and pleasant this evening.

1903

January 1st ...cleared up the front of the house. Dig up the ground around the bulbs. Went up town...but PO was closed – very tired tonight – Mrs. Mitchell and Rev. Keyes called also her niece and Susie and Margery Sheppard. Dull day. Philip throat is bad & fever high.

George and his helpers worked on the property several days, building a porch on the house and building walkways. Lambert M. Ware and his folks, and the Dotys all called on the Wests. The Bryan lots he had purchased to the east had a house on it and George had ceilings installed. Philip still had some health issues and George worried about him.

By January 12th George had to make plans to go back to Chicago and he called on friends before leaving, particularly Mrs. Mitchell, the Dotys, Sheppards, and John R. Thompson.

Back in Chicago, his colleague Mr. Gordon and Mr. J. E. Griffin were in more talks with George about a railway line into St. Andrews. They all wrote letters and contacted investors about raising the estimated $700,000 it would take to build the line. George wrote to William Hatten and to Lambert Ware about the opportunity. Ware wrote back on March 15, 1903.

My dear Mr. West,

Your favor of February 24th came duly to hand as I was on eve of starting for Pensacola to negotiate sale of my lumber contract and mill property to the Gm. Am. L. Co. (German American Lumber Company). I have since closed the trade, so am now out of the mill business. This change however does not lessen my interest in seeing a RR built to St. A. from some point north....

It appears to me that there is quite sufficient business interests existing and easily susceptible of rapid promotion to justify building a road say from Dothan to Wewahitchka or even to Apalachicola by way of St. Andrews. With deep water here and RR connection with Chattahoochee at Wewahitchka, Apalachicola's lumber interest would be at our mercy as lumber could be manufactured at Wewa and shipped from here more easily and profitably than at Apalachicola....

I think Dothan would be the best connection we could have with a short line and that the line should go around North Bay and on to Wewa and Apalach with branch in to St. A (Andrews). Two short lateral lines, one in direction of Vernon the other towards the Chipola, would make the main line to cover the naval Stores interests. A terminal at any point between Millville and Big Oyster Bar Point would be all right, though I consider Brown's tract of several hundred acres embracing Dyers & Big Oyster Bar Points as the best place. Switches and wharves could radiate from a line run in there as would the spokes from a hub and two miles of frontage be made available without the use of a single reverse curve these conditions cannot be found at any other point on the Bay.

In reference to hotel sites I do not think the East end of my tract to be the best. Though would be glad to help promote the location of a hotel in that vicinity.

Capt. Ware wrote on that he was in communication with J. P. Williams Company, G. R. Harrison and others owning extensive real estate interests in the vicinity of the Bay. He also secured statements from the German American Lumber Company covering 25 million feet of lumber, valued at $375,000 that would be shipped by rail annually, and from the Naval Stores $310,000 in value would be shipped. In closing he wrote *"The German American Lumber Company will soon build a Tram road out from Watsons Bayou through the Gay Tract"*.

After weeks of working on this, it was apparent they could not raise the money. George became seriously ill, feverish and weak. He called his doctor, but could not reach him, then, called Dr. Smith. She came and gave him medicines and instructed him to remain in bed. It took several weeks for him to recover, and he continued working throughout this time. He did manage to rent out the house in Escanaba.

In June Philip wrote George from St. Andrews, and said his grandma (Dell) was not well. Her condition worsened through the summer and George went south on August 3rd. He left on the *Tarpon* from Pensacola on the 4th, but no chance for a berth, so he sat up most of the night and enjoyed the ride. Grace and Philip met him at Ware's Dock at 8:15 AM on the 5th.

He tended to Dell, picked ¾ bushel peaches from his trees with Grace, bought clothes for the children, and went bathing in the bay at night. He hired a man to put an ice box in the house. Once completed, he got ice from the *Tarpon* when it came in again. He worked at the sweet potatoes, peanuts, and building a cistern.

George stayed until August 21st when it appeared Dell was gaining. He left at 4:00 PM on the *Tarpon,* but his berth was on the hot side of the boat and he did not sleep. The ship arrived in Pensacola the next morning at 5:00. George took the train from there and was back in Chicago on the 23rd.

August 23rd Clear – warm after sun up. Awful dusty and dirty....go in to Chicago. In at 6 – mail letter. Meet Rutherford and Jackson at Chicago Heights....feeling of loathing and disgust at the work and city life and all – wish I were out of it.

He was only back at work a few days when the message came from St. Andrews that Dell was worse and to come at once. He wrote: *"The saddest message to me of all my life – how can I bear it all – and how hopeless."*

This trip on August 30th he went by train to Defuniak Springs and from there to Point Washington where he found a man with a horse and buggy to take him to West Bay. From there he got a boat to take him home. He found that Frank and Grace had been at Bay Head looking for him to arrive there. Dell was weak, but otherwise not looking bad. He called in the doctor, tended to the house, and went up town and got provisions.

The family witnessed the 1903 Florida Hurricane on September 13th. The storm had struck the Bahamas, then crossed Florida near Fort

Lauderdale, and moved into the Gulf of Mexico. George recorded the barometric pressure beginning at noon. It fell 26 points to 29.40 by 1:25 PM. At 2:00 PM it was 29.30 and the NW wind was blowing 60 - 70 miles an hour from George's estimate. At a little after 4:00 PM he recorded the lowest pressure at 29.09, and at 6:15 PM it was 29.15, on the rise again as the storm passed. The 29.09 reading converts to about 985 millibars. The storm had come in to the panhandle between St. Andrews and Cape San Blas. Limbs were down everywhere, the grape arbor was down, and the big old hickory had twisted off. For days he cleaned up the debris and tended Dell. The Baker family helped out and took Grace and Philip on a Sunday afternoon outing to the Gulf.

On September 25th George hated to leave, but felt he could go back to Chicago, and he needed to so he could work and earn some money. He left on the *Tarpon at* 4:15 PM. He talked with Capt. Barrow as they glided through the Gulf. He had a stateroom on the ship but it was too hot to sleep. They arrived in Pensacola at 4:00 AM, and George was up at 5:00.

Dell was holding her own in St. Andrews, but Philip battled typhoid fever. George was in Chicago, worried and blue, and wrote *"Feel restless. Wish I could get hold of something to make something out of"*. Work was busy and stressful as usual. On December 12th George treated himself and bought a telescope. A few days later he wrote to his boss, Mr. Kilgallen, about taking off work and *"going home"*, meaning St. Andrews.

Dell's lungs began to "fill" and she had pleurisy. December 21st George boarded the train for Florida, and arrived at Brackins dock on the 23rd. Webster Doty met George and took him to the West home. George found Dell up and better than he expected. Philip had recovered from typhoid fever, and had killed a pig. He and George dressed it and made sausage.

On December 24th the family had their Christmas tree in the kitchen with many nice presents for all. The next day Dell made 2 pies for the family dinner, but took ill with her pleurisy symptoms at midnight. The next few days were cold and rainy. Between keeping wood on the fires, George picked up the pecans that had dropped from his trees, worked on the flower garden in front of the house, and burned the brush pile.

December 31st Clear – Temperature 38 …calm – Got at the side board – table – then stove. Got it blacked and up at 2 – uptown this evening PO…Have got 2 loads wood today. Pd Wes Gwaltney 3.50…A beautiful day in every way – wrote Mr. Kilgallen. Several nice days – 80 out in sun today. Feel quite well. Thus ends 1903. A perplexing year at times – much sickness – Plenty of work.

1904

Most unfortunately there is no known diary for 1904. It is known Dell passed away February 19th, 1904. Dr. Booth and Dr. Mitchell certified her death from malassimilation. She was 55 years old. A. H. Brake was the undertaker and he issued a letter certifying that the body was properly prepared for burial, in a sealed casket, and the deceased had no infectious contagious disease so her body could be transported back to Brandon, Wisconsin. She was interred in the West family plot at Brandon Cemetery next to Ernest Warren West, her infant grandson, twin of Philip. George received more than 20 letters of condolences and sympathy from many friends and family members. Eleanor Brown, Nellie's mother, and grandmother to Philip and Grace, wrote that Philip and Grace lost "another mother". Most people wrote how her years of suffering from physical ailments was over and she was at rest. George received a letter from his friend Luella Simmons. She wrote:

My Dear Mr. West,

When they told me that Mrs. West was dead I wanted to do for you what you did for me.... And while I know your trial is a terrible fact too real for human sympathy to touch, still I am writing to tell you that I have thought of and prayed for you in this hour of death's sad visitation.

Very sincerely, to a friend, Luella V. Simmons

1905

George had not only himself to think of, but his grandchildren entrusted to him by his daughter-in-law Nellie at her death in 1898. The year opened with George boarding at Miss Blanche Simmons' house in Chicago. Grace was 13 years old and in St. Andrews much of the time, possibly in the care of Mrs. Mitchell. Philip was 16 years old, going to school, and working some on the railroad, sometimes with George. Philip boarded at a different house in Chicago, though he frequently stayed overnight with George. In spite of the amount of moving around and disruptions in their lives George made sure the children were presented a variety of opportunities to experience.

While recovering from the loss of Dell, George began planning his business venture in St. Andrews, the Gulf Coast Development Company (GCDC). He had created circulars to mail out to prospective stockholders and was frequently meeting with people about it, and with others about selling their land in Harrison (later became Panama City) to his GCDC. The first money to come in for shares was from his friend Will Look on January 21st, 1905. The company was not even incorporated yet. George researched the Digest of Corporation Laws to determine in which state he would incorporate. He selected South Dakota. His salary on the railroad was increased to $175 per month and early in the year he began to question how long he would remain with the railroad. He needed to devote more of his time to the development company, the children, and the new woman in his life, Luella Vernette Simmons.

Speculation about the pair had already reached Philip's ears. Luella was born in 1863 in New York. Her family moved to Iowa when she was 2 years old. She was an outstanding educator and school administrator during her career. At the age of 29, in 1892, she set out on a mission trip on horseback, venturing into the remote areas of Montana to evangelize the miners and ranchers. It was said most men would not have survived the physically arduous conditions she endured. Many times she travelled alone in the Montana countryside to reach the scattered ranches and mines. This successful mission lasted 2 years. She returned to teaching for another 4 years, and then was appointed by the Governor of Iowa as a delegate to travel and study in Europe for a year, investigate, and report back to the State of Iowa on the European educational systems. She studied in Berlin and toured Italy. After the year abroad she returned to the states to teach German and Science in the high school at Chicago Heights and in 2 years became Principal there.

February 4th Clear – warmer – Did not sleep very well. Philip has bad cold in his head. Recd letters from Julia and FHL (Frank Lathrup). Wrote FHL long letter. Feel quite enthusiastic after get up about my plans – but feel depressed early mornings. Philip comes in at 3:45 to go to city. Has heard rumors and is shocked. Walk with him a little and talked. He is calmer as he starts for city – I feel the shock more than he – of his feeling so – No appetite tonight – used up.

February 5th ...Philip is feeling all right today. Talks all right and manly. Feel much better. Urge Luella to go south.

February 6th ....Philip comes down at 3 – Got him pants and we get valentine. Take supper – Enjoy our being together...

February 16th George arrived in St. Andrews. Luella was supposed to have gone with him, but she was home "sick abed". In St. Andrews George rested well, had a good old fashioned breakfast of cakes and sausage and eggs, and found the place looking in good order. He met with J. H. Drummond and others about the Gulf Coast Development Company opportunity. R. L. McKenzie took 500 shares immediately. George took some time to talk with Grace and share the news he was to marry Luella.

He headed back to Chicago on February 25th, and had a quiet night ride on the Gulf aboard the *Tarpon*, and then took breakfast on the ship before getting off in Pensacola to catch the train north. When the train stopped in Birmingham George met with friends there and signed up 2 more stockholders for the GCDC.

In Chicago he met with Jackson and went over the proposition. Jackson agreed to take shares of stock and the position of President of the GCDC. With checks in hand George went to First National Bank and opened up the company's affairs there. He wrote letters to railroad companies in the southeast, including Seaboard Airline, trying to initiate interest in a railroad to St. Andrews Bay. George involved Philip in his business, going over abstracts with him.

The development company needed as much land as could be had, and George corresponded often with John R. Thompson, Tax Collector, and obtained lots from the tax sales.

He ended his boarding with Blanche Simmons on May 20th and with little fanfare married Luella on June 1st at 7:30 AM. George was 59 years old, raising his grandchildren, and Luella was 42.

Luella Vernette Simmons West GMW Collection, BCPL

June 1st Clear – getting warm. Got married 7:30 AM. Had breakfast with folks. ..I take in rolls (to the railroad). Slept on floor again last night. Philip delirious at times...Got him some beef and port wine...

Philip had frequently been ill throughout his life and the trend continued. He had been down with Dutch Measles in May on a trip to Brandon with George. In November he was "bad with jaundice" for unknown reasons.

Grace returned to Chicago from St. Andrews on June 20th and George commented she looked well, but tanned. He found a house for the family, behind a high school. Later in June they started getting things cleaned up and settled in the house, and had their first dinner there together on June 23rd. George gave Luella the cut glass bowl he had purchased for her wedding present. In September the children started school in Chicago.

In the fall of this year George began conversations with A. B. Steele. Steele was building a stretch of railroad from Dothan, Alabama to Cottondale, Florida. George was on a mission to have him build the railroad all the way to St. Andrews Bay, construct a terminal at Harrison, and have deepwater access to shipping. Steele responded favorably after visiting the area and several meetings and letters exchanged.

November 28th ...Feel quite well on this the morning of my 60th birthday...

November 30th About 10 above zero – Blows a gale...work all engines til noon. Write several letters – Folks over to our house for Thanksgiving dinner which was very nice ...Mother Simmons, Blanche and Mrs. Mitchell – Feeling some better today. Is it the Lithia water? get another bottle tonight.

December 12th ...Go to city with Grace in PM to do some Christmas shopping...

December 24th Cloudy – snow squall over – stay in til noon – Fix up rooms – Decorate & c....Fix up tree... Mother Simmons, Blanche – Gertrude – Mrs. Mitchell & 2 children with us. Pleasant evening – All well remembered...worked engines all day. Up to office at 5.

December 31st A cloudy day. I stay at home – up to office – we work today – Feel rather depressed – Thus ends a remarkable year – and it ends finding me in failing health and being baited and goaded daily that I will quit my place – I must do so – but it seems hard to be thus down to it.

1906

There is no diary available for this year, but it is known George left the railroad and moved his family to St. Andrews in May to devote his entire attention to the Gulf Coast Development Company of which he was General Manager at a salary of $250 per month, plus 10% commission on all land sales. George had a vision for the St. Andrews Bay area. He could see the possibilities of a railroad to the bay and development of a port that would open up shipping and connect the world to this area, the gateway of the Gulf to the states. He envisioned the construction of industry, businesses, and homes. He had vast experience in the freight industry and had contacts throughout the railroad. George persistently wrote to people he knew, and did not know, reaching out in hopes of creating the partnerships that would make it all a reality. Luella settled well in St. Andrews at church and socially.

George (right), Luella, and unidentified people on a boat, GMW Collection

1907

Gulf Coast Development Company, under the management of George, was aggressively pursuing improvements for the area to increase the attractiveness to new purchasers and investors in the area. The school was constructed facing a particular direction and the windows in certain position to the desks so the students had the optimum lighting. In February this year, classes were held in the new "modern" Panama City school constructed and furnished by GCDC. The teacher's salary was also paid by GCDC. In the first 5 month term 33 students of various ages attended.

George established the Panama City Pilot newspaper and in July the Pilot front page featured its new office just east of Harrison Avenue. The Gulf Coast Development Company constructed the 1,000 square foot building in downtown Panama City. The Panama City Pilot was published there and also commercial jobs for businesses, organizations, and individuals. The Pilot published for free all the legal notices and advertisements for the Cities and the County. A building was also constructed for the Gulf Coast Development Company in downtown and a dock which the company later sold to Panama City for a third of the cost.

nama City School; First Term began February 7th; Closed June 26th, 1907; Miss Frederica R. Payne, Teacher.

Supervisor.   Teacher.

Panama City School, BCPL

Panama City Publishing Company, downtown Panama City, 1907, GMW Collection, BCPL

Gulf Coast Development Company, BCPL

Gulf Coast Development Company on left and Gulf View Inn on the right. The foot of the GCDC dock can be seen between the two. BCPL

GCDC dock at the end of Harrison Avenue, Panama City, Florida, BCPL

After years of George trying to attract a railroad to build the line from Dothan to St. Andrews Bay, A. B. Steele was committed. The June 13th, 1907 Pilot outlined the plans of Steele, and that he named the terminal location Panama City, instead of Harrison. The Panama City Pilot of July 2nd, 1908 was devoted to the grand opening of the rail to Harrison at that time and includes the history of how it came about.

The Panama City Publishing Company was incorporated November 20, 1907 for the purpose of publishing newspapers and commercial job printing.

1908

George recalled the timeline of events that led to the Panama City he was promoting.

From the January 23rd, 1908 PILOT:

S. J. Erwin, of Jackson County, in 1882 bought of the government the lands upon which Panama City is now being built. He lived in a house standing nearly where the Gulf Coast Development Company's office now stands. Early in the year 1887 G. W. Jenks purchased this property from Mr. Erwin, and selling a portion of the same to C. J. Demorest, the two platted it under the name of Park Resort, which was changed to Harrison in 1888. The hotel was then erected by G. W. Jenks, the store building by Demorest, and some sales of lots effected. With the hard times following the panic of 1892, and the death of the St. Andrews boom, the prospective city became dormant and was soon without inhabitants except Mr. Jenks' family. Conditions remained unchanged until in 1905 G. M. West, for the Gulf Coast Development Company, purchased the interests of the owners in the town site, and the following year having effected a contract with the Atlanta & St. Andrews Bay R. R. to make their terminus, replatted the property, the name being changed to Panama City, Mr. A. B. Steele, president of the railway being its sponsor.

Between 1906 and 1916 the Gulf Coast Development Company, under the guidance of George West as General Manager, made significant investments in the St. Andrews Bay area. The Bank of Panama City located on Harrison Avenue was the first brick building constructed downtown and GCDC offices were upstairs at one time.

Later, 6 acres were donated for construction of the Panama City School that opened in 1914. The GCDC gave A. B. Steele 25% of the company stock and $50,000 worth of land on the waterfront for construction of the railroad, the terminal, and necessary railroad shops. The GCDC also invested financially in the St. Andrews Ice and Power Plant, Cotton Compress, constructed the Womans Club building in downtown Panama City, and the Gentlemen's Club House. The company built docks, dredged channels, gave the land and constructed the water works and paid for the wells, which it sold to Panama City significantly below cost. A city block was donated for construction of the court house after the GCDC had provided the $400 to have Washington County divided, created Bay County, and made Panama City the county seat.

Land for churches was donated to Baptist, Methodist, and Catholic congregations for construction of their buildings. The land was donated for both white and colored churches according to George's writing. Land was donated and part of the construction cost given for construction of a Presbyterian Church. Oakland Cemetery was created from GCDC land and $500 invested in it. Sidewalks and roads were paid for by GCDC. They also aided the city by purchasing bonds when Panama City was strapped for cash.

The Gulf Coast Development Company was financially behind the construction of the Ice and Power Plant and dock at St. Andrews just west of George's property. He understood what was required to attract business and residents to the area and he had a plan to make Panama City a great port of entry.

In March 1908 George was away on business and Luella successfully handled the publishing of the Panama City Pilot, writing the articles "forcefully". She had frequently written for the paper before. Her last article, "A Wifes Privilege" was published May 7, 1908. Upon George's return she became ill and passed away April 30th, just shy of 3 years into their marriage. Her body was interred in the new Oakland Cemetery, which she had named. The Chicago Heights Star published this on the front page, May 7, 1908:

Death Comes to Mrs. Geo. M. West

Passed away Thursday Last at her home in Panama City, Fla.

Was a highly respected woman

Had Many Friends in Chicago Heights Who Regret Her Demise Keenly

Mrs. George M. West, formerly of this city, died at her home in Panama City, Fla., Thursday last, after an illness of several weeks' duration. The funeral services were held Friday afternoon, interment being in a plat of ground which Mrs. West had selected for a cemetery, and in which she had expressed a wish to be laid when she had passed away.

The news of Mrs. West's death, although forecasted in letters which had been received by her sister, Miss Blanche Simmons of this city, came as a severe shock to her many friends in Chicago Heights.

Was Well Known Here

Mrs. West was well known here and was much beloved and highly respected by all who were fortunate enough to have gained her acquaintance. For three years she was an instructor in the High School. During her residence here she was active in the Methodist Church, of which she was a devoted member. Three years ago next month she was united in marriage with George M. West, who was at that time superintendent of the Chicago Heights Terminal Transfer railroad, and at present secretary and General manager of the Gulf Coast Development Company, with headquarters at Panama City. About 2 years ago Mr. and Mrs. West went to Florida to reside.

Highly Educated

Luella Simmons was born in Allenburg, N.Y. She was highly educated, being a graduate of the State Normal school, at Cedar Rapids, Iowa, and Penn College at Oskaloosa, Iowa. She also took special work at the University of Chicago, and spent some time at the University of Berlin, Germany.

Mrs. West is survived by her mother, Mrs. Julia Simmons, and three sisters and two brothers – Miss Blanche Simmons of this city, Mrs. C. W. Matteson of Swea City, Iowa, and Mrs. R. O. Everhart of Portland, Me; E. E. Simmons of Roscoe, S.D., and R. C. Simmons of Roosevelt, Okla. Sharing with them in their sorrow are many friends in this city, who had profound regard for the deceased because of her gentleness of character and lovable disposition.

The Panama City Pilot published an obituary that detailed her career. Luella's marker at the cemetery reads "Though dead she yet speaketh". Surely George felt that as an educator and missionary she had touched lives and her influence would resound for generations through those she had come in contact with during her life.

September 12th Planted bulbs at cemetery this AM. Feel depressed.

Then in August a young woman from Millville, Lillian Carlisle, came to talk with George about printing an editorial to promote construction of the East Bay Canal to connect Callaway (where she helped manage her family's properties) to Apalachicola. Lillian was secretary of the St. Andrews Bay Ladies Improvement Club and she knew if anyone could get the canal dug it was George West.

He did publish her editorial on August 27th, titled "East Bay Canal, A Lady's Proposition". She extolled the economic value of such a canal and stated the Club was raising funds toward the construction. The article was signed "(Miss) Lillian Carlisle". The next issue of the Pilot was September 3rd, and the front page feature was a photograph and article announcing the first train in to Panama City. Sharing the front page was yet another article proclaiming the value of an East Bay Canal, written by Lillian Carlisle. She described St. Andrews Bay as being of such area, water depths, and protected from the Gulf of Mexico that the entire United States Navy Fleet could fit in it. She stated "the government would eventually place a Navy Yard and arsenal there". Lillian Carlisle saw large possibilities for the bay country as George West did.

Lillian and George continued to discuss contemporary topics, and he guided her in properly and effectively fulfilling her official position in the Improvement Club. They corresponded through the mail and by Lillian coming to the Publishing office in downtown Panama City. The early letters were strictly professional.

October 13th, 1908

Mr. West –
If you have space in your most valued "Pilot", will you please print this, or something like it, for us.
I saw Mr. Parker this pm – he says that it will be three weeks before he will have time to do the works for me, because, first, that he was run to death with work, and then too he did not have the "field notes" of this township.
Of course, this waiting isn't very pleasant, and if such a thing is possible, I'll go on, but otherwise, "I abide my time" –
Will be down the last of this week, in interest of history of the "East Bay Canal", if it is still your wish for me to write it up – I think that it should come out in next week's issue.

Sincerely,
Lillian Carlisle

By the letter of November 4th, Lillian is a woman in love, and apparently George was in love with her.

My Dearest One –
At last the closing hours of the day have come, I lay aside work and am alone, thinking of you and reading and rereading my "love letters". Dearest you could teach any true woman to almost worship you, just as I do, no one could resist such a true unselfish love as you give. My

most earnest prayer, now, since I am so fortunate, is to be <u>all</u> that you could or may desire.

Take me and make me what thou will, for I am yet young enough to bend and change (except my creed or faith) especially for <u>one</u> I <u>love devotedly</u>. No, I can't believe that you love me the best – now. Darling we will be so happy living a life based on respect, confidence, and truest affection oh it all looks so bright. Honest, if you were a hundred I would not give you up now. Dearest we'll just take the best care of you, and then we will have many, many years of happiness. Won't we?

Your letter is in my lap and when my eyes fall on any portion I see and feel that same true love revealed that I have always wanted and lived in hopes of "all my days". But do you know, that I do not know your name? Sister asked this morning "what her brother in laws first name was," said it began with "G" second or middle with "M" – This I knew but the other I had not the least idea. What is it dear? – if you do not tell me I'll call you the same Grace does – that begins with "G - -" ha – ha.

....Grace was very nice to us, perhaps I noticed other little things you did not of which I'll tell you later. Why not come and spend the day with me Sunday, if you are busy Saturday. But if any knew where you were going our secret would be guessed –

Do not let Grace disappoint me Friday, for mama, though worse this a.m. is better and I believe company would help her, as of course I'll play the part of good "Bridget".

I have always admired a business man, but always thought before that they never really loved or had time to love anyone and now since I have the two in one, you can't imagine my happiness. Dearest – you have made my life so bright, and when I was least expecting it. Can I ever repay or pay you - ? –

Would you believe it, I've been in here reading thinking, wishing, and writing until every thing on the place is asleep and it is after eleven – therefore I must say goodnight, with a heart and soul full of love I am <u>your own</u>,

Lillian

The letter writing continued nearly every day between the two. Only Lillian's letters appear to have survived through time. George's letters and no diary for this year have been discovered to date.

1909

George's next diary entries are noticeably different than when he was married to Adella and Luella. For the first time in any of his diaries, when George was down or blue, he wrote that Lillian "cheered" him. Never was that written about Adella or Luella. This was a perfect match. Two ambitious intellectuals attracted to each other and admired by each other. The writings show how involved she was with him professionally. He wrote often when "they" would go home from the office together or to a meeting together, and sometimes Lillian attended Council meetings alone. He referred to her as "L" in his diaries.

January 1st A new year is ushered in with sunshine and a cool breeze. Work in the office all day. Get many things in shape for closing 1908 – writing all day off and on.

January 2nd Clear beautiful day. Writing steady til 2 PM. Getting old year matters straightened out. Also charters ready for 2 companies. Go to L's (Lillian's) at 3:30. Arrive 5:15 very glad to see me – and I feel very restful. Pleasant moonlight evening...

January 3rd Clear day – restful – took stroll in woods with Ben... L feels well – a restful day – start home at 2:30 Home 5.....Grace and Philip home.

January 6th Very busy, McKenzie and Atkins prevail upon me to go to Washington – Will start Friday. Write Steele. Letter from him wants loan. My letter to L not sent from PO...Feel depressed tonight – so driven in all ways – Tired out – L down this AM from Millville cheered me some...

January 7th To office on foot. Look over the work on road. Busy day. All kinds of work – Paper off – work on argument to be made at Washington. 3:45 go to L boat. L away. Meet her on road – about 30 minutes visit. Back Panama 7:30...

George did travel by train to Washington, DC on January 8th. He and R. L. McKenzie, J. H. Drummond, A. J. Gay, and possibly others met with the Board of Engineers to discuss the East Bay Canal. George and McKenzie also lobbied for funding from the Rivers and Harbors Committee for construction of the East Bay Canal. Drummond checked the status of an appropriation to dredge the East Pass of St. Andrews Bay. The delegation spent 3 days in Washington meeting with senators and representatives to secure the projects for St. Andrews Bay in the Federal budget. On the 12th, George was on the Seaboard Airline train headed toward Jacksonville, and then home on the 14th. The GCDC paid all expenses for the delegation to Washington.

He received a letter from his Aunt Sarah and she wrote of hearing he was gallivanting at Washington, D.C. and she was surprised after his declaration to her that he had no political aspirations. George did not. His gift was in writing and promoting ideas. Aunt Sarah also reported Aunt Maria was not doing well.

January 14th Visit about Cottondale...Home at 1:50. Clear nice day...Feel better than I have in a long time – Philip at Marianna, Grace not in good shape. Must do something with her.

January 22nd Clear – out at 7:30 to (Oakland) cemetery. Have 7 men – Got 3 loads shrubbery from home. Put out 200 cannas, 80 honeysuckles, 8 spanish dagger, 4 red cedar, 20 crepe myrtles, 10 lantanas – 1 Confederate Jasmine, 6 hyacinths – Got some road cleared – 2 trees cut – ground fixed. No dinner – Home at 6:30 – Tired out – Grace has party – came to Panama City at dark – Got mail – 2 letters from L.

January 23rd Clear – warm – Much to do this AM. Many papers to go over – work til 5 when take L home – Got there after dark. Pleasant evening. Talk over plans for future & c.

January 24th A most beautiful day in every way – Roam in the woods – Rest after noon – Home at 3:45 PM

January 29th ....Philip down with me at night...Philip goes to Marianna tomorrow AM. Grace to PC with him to dance...

Through Lillian's letters it is apparent there was opposition to the relationship and on February 7th Lillian wrote George.

My Darling –
You have just about gotten home now, so I'll begin my letter.
Dearest, since you left Papa has been talking about the Buckley affair and darling he says that it is not safe to have Howard speak the words that make us one "in the sight of the world" – therefore "we are up against it" – but here is a plan. We have just a quick five o'clock dinner, you and I come out in one buggy and Mr. Look and Hastings in another – after dinner let Hastings say "...... she's yours" and we be going at once for home. Now dearest this is the best plan I can think of – of course if Mr. Look can't come you select anyone you wish, or I could get Ben to go over after Hastings. Darling anything that suits you will be ok with your little girlie but I believe it would be better for Mr. Look to come. Dear, I will write Nell tonight telling her the news etc. We must

have her visit Grace this summer. Oh darling is it true there are only six more days of single life for Lillian Carlisle. But I do not care, really I wish they were over now – but I'll not write more tonight. Dearest decide which plan we'll act upon and write me.
Lovingly,
Lillian

On February 13th, the day before Valentine's, George and Lillian married. She was 24 and he was 63. On the second page of the Panama City Pilot on February 18th, 1909, in an obscure local items column, between "Duck Hunting being tip top this year" and "W. S. Sheppard has fitted up his building...near Harrison Ave as a roller skating rink", it read:

> Married: At the residence of the bride's parents
> at Callaway, Fla. On Saturday, February 13th, 1909,
> by the Rev. J. G. Hastings, Mr. G. M. West and
> Miss Lillian Carlisle.

George recorded the day in his diary.

February 13th Misting and rainy by spells – Began to clear by 3 PM. Monthly meeting of Club. L down with Ben at noon. At 4:10 we start for Callaway. After 6 when we reach there. Rev. Hastings there with Ben, Nettie, Howard and Mr. and Mrs. Carlisle. Married at 7:30 pm. Starlight. Had a nice little supper and start home. Reach there at 11 – Frank's and Arthur's folks came over – Midnight before we get to our room.

February 14th A beautiful day – By evening wind went into SE blowing a gale. L and I staid right home all day – Restful and happy.

Some days George travelled to work by boat from his dock in front of house to Panama City. Some days he walked. Some days Lillian took him in their carriage. Being quite capable on the water, she also would sometimes take the boat and go pick him up. Often she worked at the office helping with the paper by gathering news, writing articles, and doing the press work. George was very pleased with his February 18th edition of the paper. It featured his "Old St. Joe" article on the front page. He was also covering the missing sailing vessel *Cleopatra* owned by Capt. Witherill of St. Andrews, formerly of Fond Du Lac, Wisconsin. During a winter storm the vessel was on the Gulf of Mexico and loaded with 110 barrels of rosin from St. Joe. The captain and crew were apparently washed from the deck along with the barrels. Two bodies were found on Crooked Island on February 17th, and in late March the vessel with 8 barrels of rosin on deck was found washed ashore on St. George Island. There was little damage to the vessel, and it had apparently drifted in the wind, tides, and waves around the Gulf until coming to rest in the sand on the beach. The engine was salvaged, but it was determined to be too costly to salvage the vessel from the beach where sand began to cover it over.

Another marriage was announced on March 4th. Philip told his grandfather of his plan to go Marianna the next day to be married to Margaret Betti Alderman. "Maggie" as she was known, was born in 1882, making her 6 years older than Philip. From George's diary it appears they married on March 7th. Grace was away on a trip, and returned home on the ship *Manteo* on March 9th. Lillian picked her up at the dock and then picked up George from work.

Luella's cemetery marker had arrived from Georgia, and when George opened the boxed monument, it was broken. A new one was made and shipped to Panama City.

March 15th George and Lillian travelled to Chicago, her first trip there. George had a Gulf Coast Development Company meeting with partners. It is possible this photograph of George and Lillian was taken on this trip.

Lillian and George West, c. 1909, BCPL

Home at the end of March, George hired a man to build the pergola in the backyard. George grew vines on the posts and many photographs of the family were taken here through the years. George still took time to enjoy his hobbies of going over to the Gulf by boat, looking for shells, and fishing. George wrote that he got "sunburnt" and caught no fish.

Pergola behind the West home in later years after the vines had grown. Fish pond at far end. GMW Collection, BCPL

April 19th ...Do much in office and on paper on flowers. Write til 3 PM. Surveys at work in St Andrews. No one knows who they are working for.

By April this year the St. Andrews Buoy newspaper printed what George called a wild attack on him, claiming he was neglecting St. Andrews in favor of Panama City. In reality R. L. McKenzie and George spent a great deal of time in communication with A. B. Steele about construction of the railroad spur to St. Andrews to support the flourishing fishing industry.

August 6th Stormy at noon – Went home by boat and slipped on oily plank as I jump to dock from boat. Hurt left leg badly.

George's leg took several weeks to recover and meanwhile the printing business was extremely busy and he could not slow down. Then Philip came to see his grandfather and revealed his financial state. George was shocked when 21 year old Philip said he planned to file bankruptcy and his wife Maggie had a baby on the way.

September 17th ...Will and Frank buy Red Fish Point...Tarpon landed 5:30 PM took on passengers.

There had been some disagreement between the Panama City Council and George about the dock constructed by Gulf Coast Development Company. The *Tarpon* was stopping there and the city was opposed to that. The GCDC agreed to sell the dock to the City for $2,200, a third of what it had cost to build.

Lillian continued to successfully run Carlisle family business affairs and negotiated to sell her turpentine rights on 80 acres she owned in Callaway. She bought stock in the Gulf Coast Development Company and George was a stockholder in the Bank of Panama City. She supported George in all his work, in business and at home. The remainder of 1909 the weather was very cold, to the point of hard freezes. Several nights George and Lillian stayed up into the night keeping fires going on the property to keep the citrus trees from freezing.

George's December 9th diary entry is perplexing. It is known that at some time Lillian had twins that did not survive. It is only speculation to wonder if this date was when she discovered she was expecting or lost the twins this day. This speculation comes from the understanding of how George used the word "shock" in his writings.

"...L had sort of shock this AM"

December 25th ...Got up at 6 and found tree. Fixed it. Home at 5 with Will. Have tree at 7:30. Frank's folks – Will and our folks. Sat up til nearly 11 – Lots presents – pretty tree.

December 27th Up at 2 and began 16 fires. L helping. Kept at it til 7. Then down to 25 hard freeze. Up to bank all day.

December 30th ...Firing difficult in high wind. Lambert (Bert Ware) *came at 2 AM to help. L up with me.*

December 31st ...Feel old after being up two nights.

1910

January 8th Started fires 1:30 AM. Down to 28 degrees. Kept them up til start for train with Frank at 6:45...

In Chicago George met with people, held the GCDC annual meeting, and traded, buying Lillian dresses, a hat, and shoes, and some collars for him. He left for Washington on the 12th to meet up with Jackson, Drummond, McKenzie, Gay, and Ashton. George, McKenzie, and Gay went to the White House. They all visited several congressmen and George and Drummond went before the Rivers and Harbors Committee to lobby for funding of dredging the channel at St. Andrews Bay and construction of the East Bay Canal. Drummond stayed for 6 weeks in Washington and George returned to Panama City after 5 days there, feeling confident. Lillian met George at the train to take him home.

George M. West, c. 1910, BCPL

Later in January the Wests bought a cow. Lillian paid $30 and George $20. Lillian attended the annual bank meeting with George and then they worked at the Publishing office. A winter storm gale blew through on the 28th washing boats ashore and taking down trees. George wrote he was able to hear Grace play and sing on the 30th.

In February George and Lillian set out to Land's End for a day of relaxing, and George got some help at rebuilding his dock. The good news came from Drummond that the funding for the East Bay Canal and bay pass dredging had come through Congress.

George and Lillian celebrated their anniversary at home alone together, but the next day brought the news Philip was sick and in bad shape. He had been frequently ill throughout his life, but would recover each time. Then came George's first great-grandson.

February 25th ...Feel too cold to work – but must do much. Message from Philip – Has son born to him this AM. Named George Francis (West).

George consistently had employee issues at the Publishing Company. Many times he wrote they came in drunk or did not show up. When they did return to work, George would try and talk with them and keep them employed. By April Philip arrived on the *Tarpon* after losing his job in Pensacola and with no prospects in sight. So George put him to work at the Publishing Company and Lillian also came more active in the business at this time. Philip's performance started out poorly and George had to do quite a bit of coaching. Philip was tending to drink and was getting into fights out at night.

April 16th Blow gale from SE. Heavy rain at night – Cow out and off tonight ..

April 17th Blowing gale from west – up town at 9 with boat – take up vegetables and milk …cow came back this evening.

May 19th Foggy – smoky – could not see any effects whatever of earth passing through the comets tail last night

May 23rd ….work in the bank most of day. Matters in bad shape there. Maggie and baby came down.

May 28th …down to St. A with Clark to see race. Knowles won by 4 mins….

June 30th …Order bath tub – closet and lavatory of Davis tonight. He to do gas and water plumbing at 50 cents an hour…

July 10th A quiet day – Plan on taking Grace to church when (Herbert) Wynne comes along and takes her.

In early August George and Lillian went to Chicago by train for George to conduct GCDC board business. George took Lillian to Brandon and Milwaukee, to the cemetery and to visit relatives of George. In Milwaukee they went to the home for old people to visit Aunt Maria and Mary McGrath who had just turned 115. Back in Chicago they did some "trading" to get supplies and items they wanted in St. Andrews. George also visited his doctor who said George was in good condition. They arrived back in St. Andrews, glad to be home, on August 19th.

September 15th Fearful hot – No let up this evening. Sleep on porch – paper off by 12:30. Ate up here – L brought dinner.

There are no other diary entries for the year, and George did not use a diary again until 1916.

1911

All information from 1911 through 1915 is based on the West documents collection and the Panama City Pilot.

In 1911 construction of the East Bay Canal began, using the barge *Blackwater* which became referred to by everyone as "Lillian's barge". The canal was completed and opened in 1915.

Lillian's Barge, GMW Collection, BCPL

In July, Grace was with 11 others on the launch *Secret III* owned by Ed Hand when tragedy almost struck. The party had been to Gulf Beach in the evening and around 9:30 PM was returning to St. Andrews, just off Hawk's Point (also known as Davis Point). Another vessel was traveling a course that appeared to be from Panama City to the Gulf. However, the vessel turned and headed toward the *Secret III*. Capt. Whittle turned *Secret III* to the right, and blew the whistle, but the other vessel kept coming toward him. The *Secret III* was struck on the forward port side and water came rushing into the launch. Everyone put on their life preservers and moved to the stern of the boat, which lifted the damaged hull out of the water. They grounded at Hawk's Point near his wharf, where he was watching from the beach, having heard the ladies screams and the whistle. Hawk took the party in his boat and they pursued the other vessel catching up to it about at the lagoon (Grand Lagoon). It was the *Eudora*, newly acquired by Mr. Paton of Lynn Haven. He had been asleep in the boat and his captain had not acknowledged he hit anything.

On November 16th Charles Alderman West was born to Philip and Maggie. He was the second great grandson born to George.

1912

The St. Andrews Bay Telephone Company was created with significant investment of the GCDC. George served as Secretary and expanded their phone operations through agreements with other phone companies with lines in the area. The St. Andrews company agreed to

Lillian West holding George Francis West (L) and Charles Alderman West (R) sitting under the pergola at the West home, GMW Collection, BCPL

connect its line with the line of the West Florida Telephone Company at Harrison Avenue and both would be able to use all lines to service their customers.

The Panama City Cotton Compress Company was incorporated on July 20th, 1912 by J. M. Phillips, G. M. West, and R. L. McKenize with capital of $35,000.00. The company was established to buy, sell, import, export, gin, and clean cotton; all activities associated with the seed and any by products; to buy real and personal property for the venture; and to construct roads, rail, and docks, to ship via rail, road, or water, and many more activities related to the business. The compress company was founded based on the ability to ship cotton from Georgia and Alabama once the East Bay Canal was completed. It was located on the east side of the railroad terminal in Panama City. Some other investors who purchased stock after the corporation was established were A. J. Gay, A. B. Steele, W. H. Lynn, N. R. Hays, and Gulf Coast Development Company which put up the land for a building.

On November 14th Grace West married Alpheus Baker Joyner of Gadsden County, Florida. A. B. had been previously married and had 2 sons residing in Havanna, Florida. A detailed article about the wedding and festivities was published on November 21st in the Pilot. Some of the excerpts include:

The ceremony was performed in the centre of an open heart, consisting of thousands of pink and white chrysanthemums, interspersed with wild smilax.

The bride was becomingly dressed in a gown of embroidery and lace over white satin, with her hair artistically ornamented with a coronet of pearls and orange blossom.

GULF COAST DEVELOPMENT COMPANY.

LIST OF STOCKHOLDERS.

G. M. West	2230	*person*
Enterprise Lumber Co.	1995	*proxy WJS*
R. L. McKenzie	1300	*person*
Thompson et al	500	*proxy WJS*
W. J. Jackson	500	*person*
A. J. Gay	500	*proxy RBm*
E. H. Seneff	275	*person*
H. W. Jencks	390	*proxy RBm*
A. G. Tanton	300	" *BHS*
W. F. Look	185	" *BHS*
J. E. McKenzie	150	" *RBm*
F. M. Brogan	100	" *BHS*
F. H. Lathrop	100	" *BHS*
E. H. DeGroot	100	" *BHS*
Julius C. Mason	100	" *BHS*
P. E. Follen	100	" *BHS*
Alice Kneebone	100	" *BHS*
Blanche Simmons	100	" *Jmw*
G. H. West	100	" *BHS*
D. Mulholan	100	" *BHS*
S. R. Look	100	" *Jmw*
G. H. McKenzie	87	" *RBm*
L. M. Tuthill	60	" *BHS*
J. T. Brown	50	" *BHS*
A. A. Myers	50	*not aburanted*
Bank, Panama City	40	*proxy BHS*
Francis P. Johnson	10	" *RBS*
Belle Booth	35	" *Emw*
Elizabeth Wyant	35	*not represented*
In Treasury	93	" "
R. R. Powers	5	*person*
~~S. N. McKenzie~~	~~100~~	
A. H. Perry	60	*proxy RBm*
W. C. McKenzie	50	" *RBm*
Clara McKenzie	110	" "
	10,000	
	178	
	9822	

The Gulf Coast Development Company list of stockholders, or subscribers, was updated by George for the annual report.

The presents to the bride were many and beautiful, all of which were displayed in a room in the home of the couple, the house adjoining the West residence, which was a wedding gift to the bride from her grandfather, Mr. G. M. West.

1913

People commonly used the makeshift driveway along the beach of what is known today as Beach Drive, but when the Town of St. Andrews attempted to take and improve the road, the residents along the waterfront were successful in obtaining a Temporary Injunction against the Council proceeding. Several of George's friends and business colleagues were on the opposite side from him in the case: F. Bullock and C. J. Setterlind who were on the Town Council, and John R. Thompson who was Clerk.

George founded and incorporated yet another business, the Panama City Dredging and Dock Company. The company had capital of $25,000.00. George purchased 5 shares at $100 per share in March this year. The company purchased the tug *Deo Volenta* from R. Tomasello for $6,000.00. A thousand dollars of that was stock in the company for Tomasello.

It appears George and Lillian owned a market in downtown Panama City where they sold milk, eggs, and produce from their garden and livestock. Some mornings Lillian had to milk the cow and deliver it by boat to the market. Most mornings George took it with him as he headed to work.

1914

The economy was struggling in the south as World War I began. Very few GCDC lots were sold during this time.

The third great grandson of George, Marion Rawls West was born to Philip and Maggie on November 26th. He was always called by the nickname "Bay".

In this year George and Lillian purchased the Panama City Publishing Company building in downtown Panama City from the Gulf Coast Development Company.

1915

From the West documents it is known that George gave Lillian ¾ interest in the Panama City Pilot, the subscriptions and accounts, and the equipment. The economy was depressed in Panama City and St. Andrews, and there were financial issues for GCDC and many individuals. An envelope of miscellaneous notes, receipts and deeds was labeled with George's typed note when in later years he was getting his affairs in order:

Notes paid, Mortgage that has been cancelled, loan to G. M. West by W. H. Hatten to pay up old Bank of Panama City claim. Lost through theft of O. P. McKenzie. Also the note given by Look, R. L. McKenzie and myself for $10,000.00 that went into the bank, total loss. Settled in December 1925. Total loss up to date on notes and stock owned by G. M. West in Bank theft, over $17,000.00.

O. P. McKenzie was cashier at the Bank of Panama City. He left Florida and resided in Albany, Georgia until September 1916 when he and his wife returned to Panama City.

A. B. Steele owed the Bank of Panama City $3,700.00 of which he wrote to R. L. McKenzie about working out a trade of stock or a loan. There were financial struggles throughout the year for many, especially in the south. But in the coming months more northern investors would look to the St. Andrews Bay area, as the northern cities were flourishing and investors were searching for fresh opportunities. William H. Lynn was one of those.

A railroad spur had been constructed from Panama City to St. Andrews. The depot at St. Andrews was opened in November and declared handsome, brilliantly lighted, and a picture of beauty to the travelling public.

Some pleasure also came to George, as his great-granddaughter Eleanor Rose Joyner was born to Grace and A.B.

1916

January 1st A cloudless sky ushers in the new Year and a temperature that is more fitting to June than to January. A little late to the office – Get much done in way of clearing up desk and writing necessary letters. Done little writing for editorial page. Everyone about sick with this prevailing influenza. My head and throat in bad condition. Begin again my diary after years neglecting it – wish had kept on through 1915 – which was the most eventful and disastrous year to me I ever passed through – How I keep up under it all is a mystery to me.

January 2nd Wrote a little for the paper in the morning – then to P (Parker) with Lillian – children with us. Afternoon went to Callaway – children along. Visit with Pitt and Mr. C. Mother C sick. Back home 5 PM. Play all pieces on victrola...

Mr. C and Mother C were all Carlisles, Lillian's parents. Pitt Callaway was Lillian's uncle. .

Work and daily life continued as usual for the Wests. George had started keeping the diary again and noted that there were reports of an oil well in Southport, he received money from the first GCDC sale in a long time, and he met with A. Weller of the Bay Fishery Company, a candidate to the State Legislature for Bay County. The Fishermens Union, including the Raffields, unanimously supported Weller, because he understood the fishing industry which was the most important industry at the time for the coastal area. Boats would bring in 7,000-10,000 pounds of fish and more, each trip and the fish had to be prepared and shipped by boat and rail. The fishing industry supported many bay families whether they fished, worked in the fish houses, or in maritime and rail shipping.

When not working, George and Lillian would go to the Pastime Theatre in St. Andrews near the depot, the Casino, or to the Panama and Idle-Hour Theatres in Panama City. On nice days they would still sometimes take a trip to the Gulf or Lands End in the boat. Of the great grandsons George and Charles were most often at the West home visiting and playing. Now about 4 and 5 years old, they tagged along often when their great grandfather George went anywhere. The usual problems would arise at home, such as the sewer pipes stopped up and George found roots growing in the pipe. That had to be fixed like so many other things around a house.

He was surprised by a visit from his Chicago friend and business colleague Will Hatten. Lillian had picked him up at the train and walked in with him to surprise George. Lillian may have planned this to lift George's spirits. George was very glad to see Will.

William H. "Will" Hatten,
GMW Collection, BCPL

The Pilot covered the "Temperance" parade held in Panama City on Harrison Avenue, with many cars, trucks, and wagons full of people, and 300 children walking in the parade. The parade turned on Beach Street and circled back to the courthouse where speakers and entertainment kept the crowds. The weather was cold and wet, but the attendance was still large. At home George started the fires at 7 PM to save his citrus trees in the 20 degree weather on February 2nd. Lillian took over at 10:30 PM and stayed up until 2:00 AM adding wood to the fires.

From February 12th to the 20th George was on the railroad once again to travel to Chicago for the annual Gulf Coast Development Company annual meeting. Lillian remained at home this time and worked every day at the Publishing Company.

In March George and Lillian hosted Prof. Byron W King. He visited the St. Andrews Bay area and spoke at 4 of the area school auditoriums. He was manager and instructor at his King's School of Oratory, Elocution, and Dramatic Culture in Pennsylvania. King was urged to establish a Chautauqua in the area. Lillian and her niece Dorothy went along as George took Prof. King to Lynn Haven, Panama City, St. Andrews, and Millville for his scheduled speeches. While they were in the Panama City High School, someone disabled George's auto. King joined the Wests at their home for dinner.

Also in the month of March George and R. L. McKenzie were in court being tried for "looting" the Bank of Panama City. In April both were acquitted.

The vessel *John W. Callahan, Jr.* made its first arrival in St. Andrews on April 13th. The 128' ship, built at Apalachicola of Juniper wood, had been constructed for the St. Andrews Bay-River run. The ship had accommodations for 40 passengers, and was electric lighted throughout. Hearing the whistle, many people went to the dock to see the vessel, including George. He met many of those aboard for the maiden cruise.

George and Lillian spent Easter eve at the Casino, and the boys, George and Charles came down Easter noon for an egg hunt.

A new linotype was ordered for the Publishing Company and the engine for it arrived on the *Tarpon* on April 26th. By the 28th it was set up, running, and Lillian had the honor of getting off the first line of writing, saying it was somewhat stiff but alright. She and Philip practiced on it and Philip actually doing good work on it fairly soon. George wrote that Philip was setting about 1500 an hour on it. That most likely was 1500 mats, each mat an individual letter, in an hour.

In early May George and Lillian were spending evenings going in bathing in the bay. On the 12th George wrote the paper was big that day and over 900 sent out, and by the end of May the paper had the largest amount of matter ever, mostly politics and school matters. From this reporting the political war between George and some Panama City Council members was heating up.

Mrs. Carlisle passed away in May and was interred at Millville Cemetery. Lillian's father was now alone, spent more time with his daughter and George.

In June George sold his St. Andrews Bay Telephone Company interests for $250.00, exactly what he had put in it 10 years prior. On the 6th George went to St. Andrews at 7:15 AM and cast the first vote in the elections that day. A few days later there was quite a stir when it was discovered that 2 ballot boxes had been stolen. George called it rotten business. Things continued to seem to go wrong. Philip had started working for the County in 1913. He was in charge of map filings and highway data. But he was prone to drinking at work. Lillian lost her cameo pin she always wore.

Pressing forward in life amidst the setbacks, Lillian and George hosted 16 girls for a watermelon cutting and evening bathing in the bay. George picked up his genealogy papers again to complete those. July 1st George printed and sent off his first weekly issue of the Chicago Daily Pilot. Lillian had secured 100 subscriptions to the new paper. This paper about the St. Andrews Bay area was for the investors and interested parties from the Chicago area. As of this writing there have been no issues of this paper found. The Panama City Pilot became a daily publication in July. The new linotype was promoted in the paper.

July 5th ...storm came from Swan Island...Storm at its height or tide is. Destroys beach road in Panama City up to Old Town bridge – Docks all gone or broken up along beach from RY (railway) dock to Old Town... within two feet of tide of 1906. No reports from anywhere as yet – Beach covered with debris up to West End after news this AM...

This hurricane hit Gulfport, Mississippi on July 6th with gusts up to 104 MPH. The surge damage extended through Pensacola and apparently to St. Andrews Bay based on George's account.

Philip missed more work being out from drinking. The final bank case against George and R. L. McKenzie was finally dismissed, but not without a threat from States Attorney Ira Hutchison, saying he would get a Grand Jury to bring more indictments against West and McKenzie.

September 2nd ...Closes with one of the heaviest thunder storms of the year – or many years. Lightning grand – Burns out generating at the power plant.

September 11th ...Over to Gulf tonight with L and 20 St. Andrews young people. A beautiful night but cool. Home at midnight. Lunch at pavilion – dancing and out on the beach...first time I have been out with a party in years.

September 21st ...appointed 3 board trustees and an advisory board of 5. Another mess by which the 1st Natl get control of load money for 20 years.

George and Lillian were fearless in reporting the news, and in 1916 the exposure of City and County business not being conducted in compliance with State Statutes made the couple targets to be quieted. On October 12, 1916 a front page article about the County Court stated the Court allowed the Sheriff to select the jurors he wanted instead of following the legal process. There had been much discussion among the citizens and the local attorneys about dissolving the County Court. The Pilot also attacked the politicians over a road construction project. The Wests said the awarding of the project to Bay County Asphalt Trust was a crooked deal, not in the best interest of the taxpayers. There was also evidence of corruption in the selection of Board of Bonds Trustees. George called out the council for its appointment of board trustees for the road bonds at 1st National Bank. There were conflicts of interest and George wrote, and the statutes stated, council members benefitting in purchasing and services for the city were illegal. Later, the Wests reported that the road bond money accounting was not being reported as required by law. $100,000 was spent from the bond fund, with no accounting provided to the taxpayers.

George wrote to his friend W. J. Jackson that he believed his property and life to be under threat. He wrote Jackson about the exposed "construction tryst" having angered the Panama City Mayor against him.

October 2nd ...had the fight all on my hands – worn out – Action of the board making appointments rescheduled...L at the meeting all the PM. Been 10 days of a hard fight. Have done my best.

October 13th Phone call at 2 AM says Pilot office is burning. Go up at once. Nothing left. No water - appears to have been set on fire in back part – Go to St. Andrews and wake up DeBroux. Arrange to issue paper from that office today. Got boys and start about 8 AM. I work at it about all day – Wire both papers off at 6:45. Deliver at PC by 7:15. A hard days work. L between PC and St. A many times.

The fire was observed around 1:30 AM. The night watchman, James Lewis, said he was by there around 12:30 and did not notice anything unusual. George wrote in the Pilot that the entire building was engulfed as if gasoline had been poured throughout, and the water pressure from the City's system was for some reason too low to even keep the adjacent building from catching fire. George and Lillian were not to be stopped. They headed back to St. Andrews and by 3 AM secured use of "The News" office and equipment to print the Pilot. "The News" was the St. Andrews Bay News a printed weekly started in 1915. Bee Brooks, District One Commissioner for Washington County, owned the equipment where the News was printed by DeBroux. Two weeks after the fire, George and Lillian purchased the equipment and The News from Brooks for $900, George received ¾ interest and Lillian ¼ interest. The Pilot went back to being a weekly paper and the Wests took over the weekly St. Andrews Bay News. The News was printed on Tuesdays and the Pilot on Thursdays. Eventually they secured a location downtown where the Pilot was printed, and the News continued to be printed in St. Andrews.

The Tampa Times picked up the story about the fire, as did several other papers in Florida. There had been many recent incidents of newspaper editors being harassed and intimidated for reporting illegal actions and corruption taking place in government. The newspaper editors were standing up for their rights to report the facts to the taxpayers.

Amid the disaster the 4th of George's great grandsons, Philip Brown West, Jr. was born to Philip and Maggie on October 15th.

October 18th ...hurricane strikes us – Begins about 4 AM. Blows 60 miles or more an hour at 8 – L drives through it and gets boys down from PC...

153

This hurricane formed in the western Caribbean and moved over Yucatan, then turned north into the Gulf of Mexico and hit Pensacola. Before the weather gauges were destroyed the winds were recorded at 114 MPH there.

October 26th Been getting up the addition to building for linotype....and I am tired. Many letters and messages sympathy.

October 27th ...Down to St A at the building... Am informed plot is laid to kill me and man secured to do it. L and I head the movement here – Others backing them – Wire Will (Hatten) to see if he can come down...

November 28th ...My 71st birthday – Remembered by few...

December 2: 28, cold... Settled Brooks mortgage this am. Borrow $300 Bank of St Andrews 90 days – GCDC stock 100 shares collateral. Now paid Brooks $333.98 $200 $5 on $900 due.

December 31st ...to Dotys in AM. To Callaway in PM. Roads awful. George and Charles came down this noon. Went with us. Cooler tonight. Thus closes a memorable year. Disastrous upon disastrous. A fight for existence – and I am still in the race. Losses heavy and lawyers fees something fierce. I hope 1917 will be an improvement over 1916.

1917

There is not a diary for 1917, but some information is available from the West documents.

George and Lillian together purchased a "certain printing outfit" owned by A. J. Gay, and located in Albany, Georgia. The printery was being operated by G. P. McKenzie. Gay sold the equipment to the Wests for $2,500 and it was shipped to the St. Andrews plant.

In May a hand written letter came to George on letterhead of the City of Lynn Haven.

Dear Sir,

A Panama man was here this morning and while the subject of newspapers was being discussed he stated that he had got onto something that the Panama people were going to do to eliminate you from Bay Co. I asked him if they were going to kill you, he said no – but about as bad. He said it would surprise everyone when the stunt was brought off...I thought I would put you on your guard in case there was anything in it – there is a bunch at P.C. who would hesitate at nothing and I guess you know pretty well who they are.

Yours truly,

R. W. Beach, Sr.

1918

January 1st Clear, 14 degrees, snow of yesterday here. The New Year begins with the coldest night of the past three – Sunday 21 – Monday 16 – this AM 14 (degrees). An awful freeze – write early. To Panama at 11 – Back on train – Home at dark and find Aunt Anna badly hurt by board giving way at back door.

January 2nd Still cold, 28. Cow gone – Roy fixed burst pipe. Aunt Anna fell last night back door and hurt her side. Dr. Wells called – up til 12 – ugly letter from FHL (Frank Lathrup).

January 4th ...Up to office and worked at letterheads for office use – Got off 500...

January 5ᵗʰ Light storm from off Gulf today... Arrange for loan to put up printing office...

Once the St. Andrews Bay News office (R) and the newly constructed Panama City Publishing Company building (L) adjacent, early 1920's. BCPL

This was the first indication of the building to be constructed at 1134 Beck Avenue in St. Andrews to house the Panama City Publishing Company. The vacant lot was adjacent to the St. Andrews Bay News office. Most likely, this wood frame building was the location of the St. Andrews Bay News. The Wests added on to the back of this building to accommodate the additional printing equipment from Albany, Georgia. In this later photograph the Panama City Publishing Company was already constructed and the wood frame building had a new use as a store and gas station.

January 7th S wind – Gulf booming. Write news up and work at office all day clearing up...Badly crippled up. Bones ache bad.

January 11th 48 degrees, Warm, SE gale – at 2 began to blow about 90 miles an hour – changed to SW and W about 3 – Blew down trees & c (such) about 5. An awful rain and storm...

January 12th 12 degrees, High wind kept up all night – Coldest since 1897 when it was 11...

January 13th Freezing hard all day not up to 30 degrees. Light wind...Do nothing today but keep fires. Used up half load wood 2 fires.

January 14th 36 degrees, Wind SE Growing warm. Began to blow hard and rain by 2 PM. At PC til then – By 6 it was blowing a gale. At 8 PM shakes the house bad.

January 17th 30 degrees, NW wind – very chilly – Slept very well. Papers off late – L not home until nearly 7 – Cloudy and chilly.

On the 21st it snowed in Panama City. Then the news came of finding the body of A. D. Weller, Jr. on Crooked Island. He was a casualty from the wrecking of the smack *Annie & Jennie*. The vessel had left the dock on January 7th and immediately ran into trouble outside the east pass. The January 22nd St. Andrews Bay News featured the entire account from the 2 survivors of how the waves from the stormy weather had crashed over the boat and then slammed the keel onto the bottom in the shallows, breaking up the vessel from above and below. Several hours at about 1:00 PM Odom Bishop and Dewey Melvin were cast onto shore 15 miles from the wreck. They made their way through the woods on Crooked Island until they found the house of Leonard Raffield that night where they slept. The next morning Leonard was leading them to his cousin Cullen Raffield's place and went ahead to get Cullen. The 2 came through the woods in Cullen's Ford and took the survivors to Cullen's place for breakfast then on to St. Andrews. Over the next 2 weeks the bodies of the captain, 2 crew, and young Alfred Weller were recovered. On February 5th the paper featured a poem in tribute to Weller who did not survive. The author was only recognized as "H".

A load of 15,000 bricks was brought in to Ware's Wharf. It was the order placed by George for construction of the new printing plant in St. Andrews, adjacent to the St. Andrews Bay News office he and Lillian had been using since the fire in 1916. Mr. Welch and Mr. Radford went to work for George, moving the bricks off the wharf and to the building site.

March 2nd ...In PM to Millville to launch of the ship. Stops on ways after moving 50 ft...

This ship launch was the first of its size for St. Andrews Bay and George covered the story in the Pilot.

Leonidas Launching

Thousands Visit Shipyard Saturday Afternoon

...from this came the organization of a Ship Building Company, and the building of the vessel that has been christened the Leonidas, at the company's yard at Millville. On Saturday last some 2,500 citizens of this county, with some from other parts of the State, were on hand, to witness the launching of this first vessel to be built upon St. Andrews Bay. Although at 4:45 all was in readiness for the vessel to take the water, through some tightening of the track at the foot of the ways the

cradle on which the boat rested jammed when it had moved some thirty feet, and up to last night no launching had yet been effected...

The vessel is a four mast schooner, 217 feet over all and a 39 feet and 10 inches beam. She is equipped with two large Fairbanks-Morse engines driving twin screws.

The ship did get off the ways and by April 11th a trial run was scheduled.

George worked on his new book draft, *St. Andrews, Florida*, paid Lillian's gas bill of $12, and Lillian had a new engine installed in her car. J. H. Drummond and George attended the Old Settlers meeting in Lynn Haven and both were guest speakers about local history. George was elected to the Executive Board. Young George and Charles frequently stayed with George and Lillian. Lillian became very successful in selling the GCDC properties, of which George got a commission. George also got busy planting his garden at home, and at his farm near Oakland Cemetery.

Seated L to R: Marion, Phil Jr., and Charles West; Standing: George Francis West, Photo Courtesy Buddy West, BCPL

March 24th After cow 6:30. Post had her shut up with many others to get manure – To Dotys...Col. has bad night.

March 31st 51 degrees, clear. Change clocks 1 hour ahead – Cut two baskets roses L to place on her mother's grave....

April 2nd ...Garden about ruined...Another heavy rain fell this PM. Flooded everything. Feel despondent.

April 3rd ...Got 35 barrels cement...in on Tarpon – Welch drew it and 2 loads brick (up to the new building site on Beck Avenue).

April 5 ...Wrote Lighthouse people about lights out on range at harbor entrance.

April 10th ...L trades for another Chevrolet – Gets it this PM...

April 24th ...wired about brick – order 12,000...

May 12th ...Put on Palm Beach suit... George had one of the new stylish suits that were a lightweight, cooler fabric, and light colored, more suitable for the Florida weather.

May 26th Up late – wore new suit – to Dotys – Col. very weak ...Wrote on Florida history – George and Charles down...

On May 28th the crew broke ground on the new building and began digging trenches for the footing. Up to 15 men worked on the building at any time and some names George wrote down were Rogers, Stephens, Cook, Will Haines, Ed Roach, Filey Gwaltney, S. S. Wynn. The first day they got the front and halfway up the north side, which was adjacent to the railroad tracks. June 3rd was a landmark day as the crew began laying brick for the first brick building constructed in St. Andrews. George was there early. In just 3 days they had the side walls up to the bottom of where the windows would be, and 2 days later the masons were on hold until the window frames arrived.

June 21st Down to work 6:45. Hard at the building. Good foreman – Not feeling well – In bathing at night. Grace came today on Tarpon from Apalach.

June 22nd ...Will Hatten walked in upon me at 2 PM. Glad to see him.

The June 25th St. Andrews Bay News featured this on the front page:

WALLS COMPLETED

The walls of the first brick building in St Andrews the Publishing Company's plant adjoining this printer were completed at noon on Saturday last and this week the carpenters have taken over the work and are putting up the roof. This brick work under the charge of Contractor J. H. Rogers of Panama City some 220 feet in length by 15 feet in height with 24 openings was put up in 350 hours This may be considered a pattern for future work and Contractor Rogers may be congratulated upon the speed obtained.

George's diary entries best tell the story of the construction of the building:

July 2nd ...Getting in press foundations today...

July 4th ...the first one I ever remember that I did not celebrate in some way.

July 5th ...Getting in cement foundations and putting on roof – watch the work.

July 11th ...finish the flooring.

July 12th To PC. Putting in windows today – Got weights…

July 16th …cementing press and store room.

July 17th …Finishing up cement work …

July 18th …Began to plaster this AM

July 24th …getting door frame made and bench made.

July 29th …Down to office. Gwaltney quits – no carpenter. To PC….Hold meeting here at house 8 PM. Drummond, Bullock, M. L. Reynolds, Weller, Cother, Philip.

August 1st ….L bargaining to sell the market

August 3rd …Trying to get someone to help on building. Got debts settled by receipts from market …

August 7th Got load stone for fireplace…Cannot get anyone to work yet

August 9th …Smith came today and at the fireplace…

August 10th …Smith finished door sills and fireplace.

August 13th …At moving the stuff from garage to new building – keep at it all day.

August 25th Feel about used up but go up to Dotys – L takes me up …

August 26th …Stephens at work. Got up some wood with other work.

August 30th …At tiling – got along better today – L's birthday…

August 31st Get at work at 7 – will finish tiling today – Paid men tonight – job done poorly – am tired out.

Sept 3rd ...Straighten up in new building some...

September 20th ...Philip set up motor for small press in new building. Got it running in good shape...

October 7th J. L. Davis began carpenter work on office this AM. Get up light wire boards...

October 9th ...getting on wall board..

October 14th ...Davis not at work til 8 – Keep at ceiling all day...

October 15th ...Helped on office ceiling today and finish it. To PC at 4 – Tired tonight – Flu still gaining – Drummond down (with the flu)...

October 19th At moving – got over linotype and engine and set up...

October 21st ...start field work in new office. All moved but old big press.

October 22nd Rainy. Busy on paper – Painting ceiling & c. Feel this grippe or whatever it is – To PC at night for clothes – by Beach road and about used up pushing car through sand.

October 24th ...No cement yet – no wood – Got desk and filing cabinet from PC office.

October 25th ...L has fearful headache all day...

November 1st ...Croft putting on alabastine this PM.

This was the mixture that was smoothed over the bricks on the interior of the building. "Alabastine Your Walls and Combine Healthfulness with Beauty" proclaimed one of the many ads for the wall coating derived from gypsum that was mined from the extensive shale beds around Grand Rapids, Michigan. The finish could be stenciled with designs, molded into relief shapes resembling tiles, and painted. The finish was sturdy, easy to maintain, and people believed it would resist harboring germs such as scarlet and typhoid fever.

November 22nd ...Eye very painful about midnight last night..Start at West genealogy again.

November 28th ...Thanksgiving and my BD. Philip, George, Charles, and Marion take dinner with us...have nice presents.

December 14th ...help L on press work...

December 17th ...Col Doty died...A good friend gone.

Col. Charles Doty had been one of George's best friends for many years. The St. Andrews Bay News featured a thorough article and photograph of Doty on the December 31st front page. He was born in Wisconsin in 1824 and was the son of Judge James Duane Doty, the second territorial governor of Wisconsin, and a territorial Representative for many years. Charles Doty was the first white male child born in the Wisconsin territory. He married Sarah Jane Webster in 1846 and they had 3 sons: Webster, Edmund, and Bradley. Bradley and Edmund predeceased their father. Edmund's widow, their son Captain Arden Duane Doty, along with his wife and 2 children resided in St. Andrews. The Colonel was interred at St. Andrews Cemetery, which is now known as Greenwood Cemetery in Panama City. George spent many evenings with Col. Doty engaged in conversations of a variety of subjects. Col. Doty also invested in George's enterprises.

December 24th ...No tree so at 4 get pine and fix it up – looks well – Philip, Maggie, and boys down – lots cake – good time...

December 29ᵗʰ …To Dotys. Webster in bad shape – drinking hard – wish could stop it…

Webster Doty, the only living son of Col. Doty, became very despondent after his father's death and drank often, and much.

December 31ˢᵗ 42 degrees, cloudy. S wind – grows mild. Get off the News late…the old year passes away with big dance here – It has been a trying year to me – one of the worst I have ever experienced.

1919

January 4ᵗʰ 12 degrees – Lowest in years. Lavatories froze in rooms.

January 5ᵗʰ 17 degrees, clear NE wind. To Dotys 3 hrs. Supper at Zadie's

January 18ᵗʰ …To Millville and PC. Flu bad at PC. Everything closed…

February 2ⁿᵈ …L to PC on truck with mail. Walks back. Philip and I at survey of bay AM.

February 9ᵗʰ …George and Charles down…

February 28ᵗʰ ….L sold 2 lots.

In March the shipyard in Millville successfully launched another vessel constructed there under the supervision of Capt. A. B. Parks. The 4-masted *Ville De Dixmude* was launched perfectly and the Pilot expressed hopes of Capt. Parks remaining in the area and producing more vessels.

Lillian bought a new auto in April, a Chevrolet Touring car from C. M. Chandlee for $850. The Bill of Sale identifies the car with engine number B 70I00. The roads of the day were terribly hard on a car. The cars frequently were stuck in mud or sand, and debris in the roads would damage the car from underneath, busting hoses and fuel lines. Pot holes would rattle parts loose. But what had been a wooded trail, and then neighborhood driveway along Beach Drive was being surfaced and more autos were using the new road connecting St. Andrews and Panama City.

By June George completed his genealogy and published "*William West of Scituate, R.I.*" The book had taken him years to write, with extensive research in libraries, and correspondence with historians in Rhode Island. He printed and bound a limited number of paperback and hardcover copies.

Even as his health was failing and his energy fading, George continued to promote the St. Andrews Bay area, writing letters and editorials to garner support for growing the railroad and shipping industry at Panama City. He explained the benefits and convenience of ships from other countries coming into St. Andrews Bay rather than to the east coast. He still believed St. Andrews Bay to be the gateway to the country.

George also still held elected officials accountable to the taxpayers. He published in his papers the amounts of road bond money being spent in the county. He also exposed the irregular activities of the railroad in delivering the gravel for the county's road construction. The county owned the rail cars, filled with gravel, and a railroad official ordered the conductor to carry the gravel to locations other than St. Andrews. W. H. Lynn, Vice President of the Atlanta & St. Andrews Bay Railway appeared before the County Commission to answer the charge, and the County Commission passed a resolution commending Mr. Lynn for his actions, against the railroad attorney's advice. George, well experienced in railroad operations, wrote that the railroad's only obligation was to haul freight for a paying customer to their chosen location, with no preference, interest, or concern for its destination. Minor C. Keith owned the railway and vast amounts of land along Panama City, Millville, and Lynn Haven. The gravel the County Engineer had directed to St. Andrews was re-directed by a railroad official to a location 2 miles north of Panama City along the Lynn Haven-Panama City road where it would benefit Keith greatly. But the Lynn Haven-Panama City road was not one included to be paid for with the road bonds. George pointed out the bond money was being used for a road other than the roads for which it was approved by the voters.

September 15th Lillian left for a trip to the mountains of North Carolina for a month. There she helped her friend Bess with her writing and mission work. George wrote to Lillian of the ongoing issues he faced in publishing the activities of elected officials. She wrote back to him *"...But don't worry – that bunch will never down us because we have strength that they know not of...will stay until next week, then they may "look out" for I'll be there and show them that the Pilot will live, also the News. I feel like I could get out three papers all by myself if necessary...Let them think we are all down and out if they want to because it will be more fun to see them awake later – Sucks Dearie, don't let them worry you..."*

Lillian returned October 13th and George left on the 27th for Chicago for a meeting of the Gulf Coast Development Company board. On October 28th he had his picture made. He returned to St. Andrews on November 7th. Just a week later Lillian fell ill and on November 17th the doctor diagnosed her as having malaria. She recovered soon enough to speak on November 23rd at the Presbyterian Church about the mountain mission work.

December 24th 30 degrees – clear – Busy in office all day except to get tree and get it in shape this AM. Nice tree – All there.

December 25th Christmas day – Pleasant – Real quiet – George down and tries his bicycle.

December 30th 38 degrees – clear – Busy in office on News – bad time – Rollers bad – Paper off at 7 – tired.

December 31st ...Quiet end of 1919 – Been a bust year to me – but have gained a little financially I think but last two or three months have had trouble in my chest – or heart – Done and am doing much work ...welcome 1920.

1920

January 1st A pretty New Years day – hard at work in paper – off at 4 – very good work and no help in Leonard's place – To PC with paper at 5. Took dinner and spend evening with Comstocks at The Villa – dinner at 6.

January 2nd ...try to get carpenter...

January 3rd Clear – 25 degrees – Calm – but biting cold ...worked in office all day...Philip set up 3 jobs – good work – Taught Roy how to lock up job for presses...

January 4th ...Clear the street between Grace's and our place – AB helping – George and Charles down...

January 5th Clear – 19 degrees – wind gone down but very cold – Ice in many places – Capt. Frank Ware begins work 9 this AM. Garage doors first. Writing for News first then help Capt all day – get garage done – awful chilly day

January 6th *Been down to 15 degrees possibly about 7(PM) last night —* *at 8 the wind went in to the south — Capt Frank and I at steps in AM and* *shed in PM. Did not go to office or write any today...*

January 8th ...Capt Ware on kitchen roof...Tyler calls in AM to see if I will *go to Washington...*

January 10th ...Bad election — PC goes against me — Too bad so much *debt.*

January 12th ...write at home til 10 — Then foot to office. L takes car to *PC for repairs. Work at office all day. Write several letters. L back at 11* *with other car and took up lot job work..*

January 24th ...To St A to take train Drummond, Frank Nelson, and I *start for Washington*

The trio met with members of congress and the Board of Engineers for the Harbors and Rivers Committee. World War I had revealed some shortfalls in the American infrastructure. The east-west railroad trunk lines and the ports they serviced on the east coast had become clogged during the war. To George it made sense to improve the north-south railroad infrastructure and the southern ports, including St. Andrews Bay, and he took that message to Washington.

While in Washington he visited the library, Smithsonian, and Botanical garden. The 1920 movie *Shepherd of the Hills* had just been released so George went to see it and commented it was too depressing.

The party to Washington returned home on January 31st and Lillian left for a few days in Richmond, Virginia. While she was away George had an accident with an old cedar stump. He was chipping away at the stump with his ax and a piece of the root flew up and hit him "a very hard blow" on the left side of his nose, under his eye. The hit nearly "downed" him.

There were some notable losses in the community at this time due to rampant influenza and pneumonia. George wrote the "doors of death were open". Margaret M. Day, wife of Henry F. Day, passed away February 19th in St. Andrews at the home of her daughter, Mrs. J. H. Drummond. Margaret Melville Smith was born in 1836 in Ransey, Canada, lived as a young girl in New York, then Minnesota. In 1865 she married a Minnesota Regiment soldier, Henry Day. They came and settled at the peninsula east of Cromanton in 1886 during the first development of this area by the Cincinnati Company. She was survived by 3 of her 5 children, including Mrs. Grace Edith Day Drummond, Mrs. Lydia E. Day Ware, and Edward S. Day, all of St. Andrews. Grace Day was married to J. H. Drummond and Lydia was the second wife of Lambert Ware, Sr.

Also Hassie Lewis Ware, wife of Clarence A. Ware passed away at the young age of 29 from pneumonia. In 8 years of marriage they had 4 children.

Daniel Campbell, employee at the St. Andrews Ice and Power Plant, 38 years old, and father of 7, passed away. His wife and 5 of his children remained confined to bed from the disease.

Charlie Cotton also succumbed to the illness. For many years he was the manager of Ware Mercantile Company, and built a large business there and in shipping. He left a wife and 8 children behind.

Early March came in with extreme weather. For days the temperatures plummeted to 20, 24, 22, and 28 degrees for several mornings. George wrote there was ice all around.

The icy relationship between Atlanta & St. Andrews Bay Railroad Vice President Walter Sherman and the St. Andrews Board of Trade was warmed a little as he met with Drummond, West, and others to settle a railroad issue. Drummond owned the "Y" at the St. Andrews Ice and Power Company. The Y needed repairs and rail service needed to be restored for the fish houses located at the dock there. The Board of Trade had filed suit, but Sherman met with the men and agreed to their terms. Shipping the thousands of pounds of fish over the A. & S. A. B. RR portion of the rail generated a large amount of income for the railroad.

The same week in March, Drummond's 2 story garage on Commerce Street (West 10th Street) in St. Andrews burned down. The cause of the fire was never determined, but George and Lillian lost a press that was stored there, and Drummond lost the old cigar factory equipment, several new cross arms and electrical equipment.

April 4th ...Took cow to Drummonds...

April 5th ...Went after cow – ran about ¾ mile chasing her – about used up...

April 7th ...Dinner at new café St Andrews...

C. Rasmussen had opened a new café called the Bay Restaurant in the Home Bakery building. A regular dinner was 50 cents and a chicken dinner was 75 cents.

April 9th Stormy, 48 degrees. About 7 a very heavy gale began from S. In west end and out toward Pretty Bayou – was cyclonish – twisted off many trees – kept up for half an hour – heavy rain ...

April 11th Clear, 48 degrees. A very fine day – worked from 8 til 4 on the rosebushes at the pergola – were in an awful tangle...

April 17th Clear, 58 degrees. Warmest morning this year. George staid here last night – slept about 10 hours.

April 18th ...Feeling better – Good nights sleep – Put on overalls.

Later in April a phone was installed at the Panama City Publishing Company on Beck Avenue. The Wests also moved the Panama City Pilot office into a new location on 1st Street in downtown Panama City. It was the old A. H. Brake location. Philip helped get everything moved. In his diary entries George distinguished the 2 locations by saying "to PC", meaning the Pilot office, and "to office" meaning to the Publishing Company in St. Andrews where the News was printed. By the first of May he was collecting orchids along Harrison Avenue and Lillian hosted 55 children at the house with George helping entertain them.

George had a bed companion in June, a "kissing bug", that bit him in the night more than once. The bed had to be completely stripped to find the critter, also called a chinch or cone-nose bug. The bites were painful.

July 3rd ...Hear Hardee and meet him. Airplanes perform – at night we put off fireworks at home...Nice parade today of autos and floats.

The celebrations of the anniversary of birth of Bay County and July 4th were combined into 1 event on the 3rd. Cary Hardee, who would later be sworn in as the 23rd Governor of Florida attended and spoke to the crowd of 4,000. A parade of automobiles and floats, ballgames, and music by the 25 piece Fort Barrancas Band was enjoyed by the large crowd. The pilots in the 2 seaplanes exhibited what they could do and were a great attraction.

July 6th Clear, 70 degrees. Warm day again – Go to Casey's and get 4 pieces 6x7 for tank – Miley and I load them – wagon broke down – delayed 2 hours. Get them here late – Take a load to the farm to fix up house there – a hard days work – Heavy lifting – (Bert) Fuller at windows & c. L gets glass and cement at PC. $5.50.

Later in July Lillian left for Ridgecrest, Oklahoma. The details of this trip are not known.

August 5th ...To Dotys – Returning see McGriff – Am afraid someone is trying to frame up false charges. Disgusted and unhappy.

August 6th ...A thunder shower from off the Gulf. Up at 6:30....Wrote L ...not feeling very good – worry kills....

August 12th ...Cher Cola plant burns 1 PM. No message from L. To Dotys 7:30 til 8:30. Wait til 10 for train – L not on.

August 13th ...up 7:30 – shave – Got papers to PC early. Quiet day. Feel fairly well. Message from L. Be here tonight – Train late in 9:50. Looking and feeling well.

August 16th To PC early – Put GCD $120 in bank this PM. Not feeling well this PM. Stay here and write on Old St. A – Supper at restaurant – Do not go to St Andrews dinner tonight at Pines.

August 17th ...Write in Old St Andrews half the day – Got some ready for next week – to PC – All quiet.

September 3rd ....write and at office AM. Getting St. Andrews history in shape to run – Feel poorly by 1 PM Home.

September 4th ...Run history 12 pages today.

The newspapers announced "*A new element was injected into politics upsetting the old grey wolves who had carried the vote in their pockets*" as women began to register to vote on September 8th. Mrs. Mary Marshall and Mrs. Laura R. Look were the first to register in Panama City. Lillian West was the first to register in St. Andrews. George was busy overseeing the installation of a water tank and pump at the house.

September 11th ...Capt Frank tore down playhouse and moving it to tank...Finished weeks installment of history and got it set up and proofed.

September 13th ...Bert and Capt Frank at the tank house this AM...Finished tank house...

September 15th ...Helped Pratt put up electric power pole this AM. He gets wire run to pump.

September 16th ...Got pump working – pumped 3 hours – valves all in bad shape in the house...

September 18th ...Pump fails to work. Tired tonight – (Ed) Masker brings in some good photos of maps – Finished another installment this AM St Andrews history – Philip set it up and I proof it.

September 20th ...To PC at noon – See Hawk – Get data on Clarks house etc – write all PM. R. L. McKenzie...May and Dr. and Mrs. Blackshear down this evening looking at moon through telescope – Rings around moon – hazy – storm reported forming last night west end Caribbean sea.

George spent time with Hawk Massalina getting information about the old Governor Clark house and history as Hawk remembered it. What George learned from Hawk became part of the "*St. Andrews, Florida*" book George published later. Hawk had witnessed the destruction of St. Andrews in the Civil War. This is transcribed as much as possible from George's handwritten notes of the interview with Hawk:

Narcisco Massalena – born on point Harmon 15th April 1842.

2nd youngest child – was seine fishing 1st remembrance – (fish) Sold Salted – Peter Parker only other fishermen – Fished and sailed on schooners between here and Pensacola – 1st 2 years dodged Yankee boats. (2?) brothers shipped on bark Restless – when war broke out was living at Harmons. Self and father to Old Town to get out the valuables as they _____ to do so for some time –

Joseph F. Massalena – Spanish subject part Spaniard – free 1818 – over 110 years old – St. Augustine to _____ – thence to _____ – thence St. A(ndrews) – worked for Col. Long – was a carpenter – Hewed frame for Capt. Loftin's at Parker – Old Peter Parker house – was here when Col. Clark was buried and aided. Hewed ship timber (oak) for Watson – for US govt – Returned to bay permanently about 1836 and first settled on Beatty? Bayou, then came to P.C. and settled on point – Fished in (gulf or fall) – In summer built houses in Old Town – About then Capt. Blood settled in Old Town and he worked for him – boat building – house building & c (such) – Capt. Blood was his guardian.

Then Mr. Long was guardian after Capt Blood left – worked for Bakers Longs and Dixons of Jackson County at Old Town. Looked after their places winters after they had gone home – until burned in 1863. Moved to Watsons Bayou 1863. In latter part 1863 moved to Hurricane Island

– called Saddle Island. Moved to _____ in 1865 – In 1866 moved to Davis Point lived there since.

Had 4 boys and 3 girls

Father died – Mother died.

End of Interview

October 9th ...Went to Bryans fish house where he had just taken in 56,000 mackerel.

October 14th L sick with cold head and throat. Bust at office. No help on paper. L helps PM. Got it off 5:45. To PC – feel used up this PM and slept an hour.

October 17th ...To Philip's at night and get fish – read Caroline Lee Hentz – Ernest Linwood – also Mrs. Keyes' poems.

October 20th Write editorial for Pilot...To PC – Quiet day – L to Villa and meets two men from Schenectady, NY. To go out with them tomorrow.

October 22nd ...L takes men to Callaway – Long Point & c....

October 23rd ....Philip gone fishing with two NY men. Get good lot fish. We go to Villa and get some of them...

October 28th ...At the paper – editorial and then at ballots. L doing press work all day...

The Wests had secured the commercial job of printing the election ballots for the county.

October 29th …At the ballots. Get them off and to the court house 6 PM. Perforate about 6 hours – L runs press – papers off to PO at 11…

November 3rd To PC for data of election PM. Do not get anything – Get up copy – Do not like elections here – Intimidation and down with the d- Yankees is the main feature – But little or no chance to get in investors from the north – with threat to do them up.

November 18th …10 PM court house was afire and burned fast.

November 19th …visit fire – Set on fire – very bad loss to the county – over $100,000…

November 20th Everything upset. Boys in office doing nothing – Philip mad – L mad – Disgusted – to PC (in the) PM – Get what facts I can about the fire. Used up at night…

The burning of the Bay County Court House was a terrible blow to the area according to George. It was a $200,000 expenditure for a new court house that the taxpayers would be burdened with funding, except about $40,000 that the insurance would pay. He felt the community was deadened morally and financially from the loss of this icon of public pride. In the Pilot he blamed systemic lawlessness that went unchecked in Bay County. Starting with whiskey making and selling, houses of prostitution, and the crimes stemming from those, he called for the reputable citizens to rise in their might and end it. The loss seemed to affect everyone, shortening tempers, and causing sadness. Everything was going wrong at the office, there was no help to work, and George was disheartened.

November 25th …Take typewriter to pieces – broken spring. Got down the Scott gun and clean it. Been sitting up in my room since

1916...George and Charles went to the circus at PC.

Some decent weather in early December brought the opportunity for George, Philip, and some others to go fishing up at Bayou George and bring home a nice catch.

December 17th ...Got Christmas tree in and on base.

December 24th ...busy day – To PC. Got L present...try to get house warm. A very cold day – Philip, Maggie, Grace, and the five children here by 7 PM – Nice tree ..I have many presents – send off cards...

December 25th Christmas a clear calm cold day – Not over 36 degrees today. Stay at home – Ache in my hip – sciatica – children here all day...

December 31st Clear, 28. Worked about house all day. To farm and put in windows. To PC 5:30 PM. Thus ends an eventful and depressing year. No sales of my own property and times growing worse. No money and all but little business – 1921 may be even worse.

1921

January 4th Write Hatten...Look's check for $25 to be credited from him on the $10,000 note. Work at office cleaning up. Order ink....Out on railway with Drummond inspect joints – But 5 out of 50 with full bolts.

January brought illness to the family again. A. B., Grace's husband was in poor condition. Lillian put him on the train to Dothan and he went to the hospital there. Doctors discovered a tumor near his heart that was inoperable. They hoped to reduce it by x-ray, but that did not work. He returned to St. Andrews on January 23rd, as Grace was on the train headed to Dothan to see him. They crossed each other at Cottondale. Grace got back to St. Andrews at 8PM.

Amid this, Philip announced he was leaving at the end of the month. He had been working for the County and at the Publishing business for several years. Drummond and George had inspected the railroad track and found many issues. On the 31st Ed Masker went out with George and took pictures of the faulty track.

The Wests put aside the problems for their anniversary day of February 13th and took an outing with several others to Magnolia Springs. There George enjoyed the wild flowers including orchids and the plentiful pink butterworts.

A. B.'s health failed all day on the 22nd and he passed away at home.

February 23rd ...to PC to select casket $135....Funeral 2:45 at house, 3 at Baptist Church St Andrews – house full – buried 4:30 Oakland Cemetery – Grace holds up well until get home – Lina with her tonight...

The first of April brought an eventful outing to Wewahitchka for the Wests and some friends. They, along with the Drummonds, and several others, in 2 autos, set out for a picnic in Wewahitchka. Drummond had a tire blow out on the Millville bayou bridge. Easing into Millville, the gear then broke. Lee Reed, one of the party, went back to St. Andrews for Ware's truck. After an hour delay they started out again. George rode 4 hours to Wewahitchka *"on bottom of the truck"*. The other car had no trouble. They got to Aldermans Camp Ground, enjoyed a picnic at the beautiful site, and then George and Lillian jumped in the other auto for the return trip.

They took another outing a few days later in Ed Hand's boat over to Cromanton with Webster Doty and some girls along. Eleanor Rose started kindergarten and Lillian took her there for her first day.

On April 19th Howell's brick storefront building on the west side of Harrison Avenue, between 2nd and 4th Street, was destroyed by fire. Howell sold Hudson and Essex autos and the 10 vehicles in the building were destroyed.

The night of the 22nd gave a spectacular display of an eclipse of the moon at 1:30 AM that George and many others enjoyed. He described the moon as coppery in color and that the stars shown in splendor during the darkened moon.

Just 3 days later the West Bay Naval Stores and Lumber Company Mill located between Dyer and Sulphur Points (west of current Port of Panama City) was also totally destroyed by fire. Caused by a hot box under a piece of machinery, the fire quickly engulfed the structure and one and a half million feet of stacked lumber. This was the most disastrous fire ever to visit St. Andrews. The mill had been taken over by St. Andrews Bay Lumber Company in August, 1920.

During May Lillian became very ill and took the entire month to finally overcome whatever the illness was and to fully recover. George's health became more precarious as his heart gave him issues, and his pulse was around 30. Dr. Zediker gave him some medicine but this heart trouble was chronic.

The Wests were embroiled in an ongoing feud with Walter Sherman, who owned St. Andrews Bay Lumber Company, Atlanta & St. Andrews Bay Railroad, and was a Director of the First National Bank. The government had seized the German American Lumber Company during WW I, and Sherman purchased it for pennies on the dollar in 1919. The Wests called the acquisition process unfair. They backed the lumber company employees when they were on strike and wrote in the Pilot that employees should have the right to work, whether union or not, and should not be intimidated or bullied by management. In 1920 the main point of growing contention most likely was the Wests' opposition to consolidation of Panama City, Millville, and St. Andrews, and Sherman's support of consolidation. Sherman got a petition together that denounced the Wests and their "yellow journalism" and requested they leave the area. The petition had no information about what the people were signing, only signature lines. Many thought they were signing up to support the sale of the West printing business. By August this year Sherman shut down the railroad spur to St. Andrews. The feud was dormant for years, until 1931 when First National Bank was closed. Sherman was the major stockholder and the closure resulted in a number of businesses going bankrupt causing much bitterness throughout the community. A month later the lumber mill and 20 homes in Millville were destroyed by fire. People believed the events were linked and the Wests published it was so. Sherman criticized the "dirty sheet published at St. Andrews" and encouraged women to stay home and let men run the town.

The political climate was heating up with the summer. J. H. Drummond attended the hearing in Maine where it was proposed to abandon the railroad to St. Andrews. Drummond wrote a thorough summary of the hearing and his argument against the abandonment which was in the Pilot on June 9th. The lumber mill workers were on strike again in Millville. Walter Sherman was on a mission to rid Bay County of the Wests once and for all. Sherman urged his supporters to boycott the West papers and not purchase any advertisement space in the News or Pilot.

June 23rd ..At paper – off at 6 – 8 pages. Barnett circulating petition for me to get out – stop writing – and every one signing it to buy out the Pilot. The crowds desperate.

June 25th ...To PC in PM. Active all along the line in clearing me out – Talk of sending a constable down tonight or tomorrow – but L objected. Nice state of affairs.

June 26th ...Feel poorly – So hot – To Dotys at 5 – Nowhere else today. Have nice ice cream. Do not write any – Figs ripening fast today.

July 1st ...Order this AM for 2,000 copies of Pilot – Growing some

July 3rd ...Feel very bad all day – Heart acts bad – slow and irregular pulse

August 11th ...News came to Drummond from Smithwick (Rep. John Harris Smithwick) of abandonment of St A tracks – Looks bad...

August 22nd ...all train service cut off this noon.

Notice had been posted the service would end on September 15th, but the Atlanta & St. Andrews Bay Railroad took a notion to end it August 22nd. No provision or notice was given to the Post Office, with whom the company was under contract to deliver the mail to St. Andrews and take the outgoing.

From the St. Andrews Bay News:

THE SCRAPPING OF ST ANDREWS

The causing of the removal of our fish industries from here imposing upon our people the most inconvenience possible in doing business here which requires railway transportation the impossibility of getting car load lots in or out of town the possible closing of the telegraph office owing to lack of business which is largely that furnished by the fish companies the shutting down of and removal of other businesses which are dependent upon the railway has no parallel in the history of this country...

Why was this done? The St Andrews Bay Lumber Company's newspaper aided by real estate dealers not interested in promoting St Andrews who thought they saw money in combining the cities of Millville, Panama City and St Andrews under one municipality with headquarters at Panama City making that the name of the new city for some two years or more have been talking of such a combination and working to bring it about. Failing in securing the approval of but a few of the citizens of St Andrews they then turned to destroying the industries of this place hoping to accomplish in that way what they had failed to do otherwise.

September 15th ...Hear this noon of Barnett – Vick and crowd taking Gilbert out and whipping him ...

September 16th ....Feel disgusted over PC mob law.

Later in September there were rumors of the Ku Klux Klan establishing a camp at Panama City. George wrote, *"This is a severe criticism of our governor, the courts, and sheriff and is not warranted. We need no self-constituted law enforcement officials...".* His appeal was to the established judicial officers to take control, and shut down the Ku Klux Klan.

October 12th ...look at butterfly gathering this PM....and other places along beach – thousands of them – Monarchs.

October 19th Clear, 72 degrees. Fine morning – up at 6:15 and begin to write at 7 – at Pilot ed. Not feeling very good. Too much work and no play.

On Halloween the Wests enjoyed a party at Mrs. Ware's. She was known for hosting many parties. But the dramatic politics continued to play out as Labor Leader John Winstanley, on a train to Panama City, was abducted from the train at Sherman (on the A&SABRR line) and taken to a remote area by Compass Lake and beaten. He escaped and was hospitalized. He recognized 2 of his attackers as deputies.

November 6th ...Capt Smith calls – Disgusted with the Sherman move. So are others...Hear of St Andrews Bay Land Company gunman that was on way down to kill me – last week – Failed to materialize.

November 7th ...must write – Good excitement over Sherman's publication. Begin to get letters and people call to express their displeasure.

Sherman's petition from June and July this year was published. The petition was for George and Lillian to cease publishing and leave town. Most of the few people who signed the petition never saw anything in writing and signed it under misleading information. Many were told it was a petition to support the Wests selling the news papers to Sherman.

November 14th ...about 8 AM as was looking out the front library window saw a dark cloud come around the SW corner of the house striking the old cedar and taking out about two thirds of the top ...There were water spouts on the bay. This cyclone here took top of an oak tree back of Mrs. J. R. Thompson's.

Men on the wharves along St. Andrews Bay reported seeing 3 cyclones come from the lagoon area, now Grand Lagoon.

In order to shut down the railroad to St. Andrews, the Atlanta & St.

Andrews Bay Railroad had claimed the spur to St. Andrews was in disrepair. In November experts were ordered by the State Railway Commission to inspect the track. Mr. Windham, Track Superintendent at Seaboard Airline, another railroader Mr. Campbell, and George West were put on the task. The claims by A&SABRR were proved false. The track was determined to be in better condition than the main line into Panama City.

The *Glendoveer* came into St. Andrews Bay in December and as it neared the docks an explosion from within the vessel sank it. The vessel was found to be overloaded with liquor it was running from Bimini to Gulf ports. The boat was raised and brought in to the dock where State Alcohol officers unloaded the remaining cargo and more than 100 citizens and George watched.

December 23rd ...To PC. Got some presents – Get tree this PM – Charles, Bay, and I – a pretty shortleaf pine. Got it up this evening and start trimming it.

December 24th ..Nice day. Very busy – To PC in PM and get last of presents – Chas and George – Phil and Bay down early. All here but Maggie and Philip who play at dance. Tree ready by 6:30. Lots presents on it. A pretty tree – I have 4 handkerchiefs – red wagon – socks & c. All home by 8...

December 28th A fine day...At house 1 til 3 getting pictures with Elmo Bullock for her article on homes. Got a large lot....

December 31st Clear, 48 degrees. House cold by night – Rev. Bryan to house tonight – go to PC. Very busy day at office getting off LH..... Feel little better – Thus ends a very momentful year – Have just about held our own financially – have lost in health.

1922

January 1st Clear, 46 degrees. High north wind. Talk til church time with Rev. Bryan who is here today – write some – Feeling better.

January 7th ...tore down old fence chicken yard – fixed old walk by it – clean some ditches. Feel very poorly by noon – Rest this PM...

January 13th ...at cemetery again today – Had Jo and 3 men – good days work – Burned off ½ of it or more – Had to fight fire hour. Kept at it and surprised to find myself better today and tonight...

January 30th ...at home all day. Got up News editorial article – not feeling well....Charles sent home – say has chicken pox.

Much of February George spent with Philip working on the GCDC affairs. The annual report was needed, the financial books put in order, and George needed help to complete the tasks. It was becoming apparent to George that his health was failing.

February 15th ....weighed 195 – Lost 8 pounds in few days, 5 pounds in two days.

February 22nd About sick each day. Heart or stomach – and liver.

February 25th Heart worse – Got different medicine from Dr. Wm Blackshear. Had a bad week of it...

In March George and Philip began work on the affairs of the Publishing Company and his income. George worked on his *St. Andrews, Florida* book getting it indexed and ready to print. He received the first 2 bound copies May 6th. George printed the book pages at the Publishing Company and sent them off for binding.

March 28th ...Circus in this AM. Went up at noon...met many old circus men who had been through the Upper Peninsula (Michigan). *To show in PM. Continuous thunderstorms – wet everything through – L took boys home – I went along...*

This was the Rhoda Royal Circus that came to town. Many new circuses started up during the prosperous time after World War I, but Rhoda's and many others failed during the sharp recession of 1921. Rhoda only toured for 4 years.

April 8th   warm day – feel poorly – To Lynn Haven early – Go with party of 15 up the creeks – Feel better by noon – Speak on wildflowers – Home at 5, L up 5:30

For Mother's Day George placed his mother's picture on the mantle and wrapped it in Confederate Jasmine. He went to Panama City and looked over the new office space there. He had work being performed to a wood structure where the Panama City Pilot "City Office" was to be located downtown at 117 Harrison Avenue.

Fishermen in front of the City Office of the Pilot, GMW Collection, BCPL

June 3rd Car works bad. Had new battery put in – no good – Tried other things – nothing doing.

June 4th Could not start car ...out to Pilot Station with Horace and Yarboroughs. Cool out there – Been a year since was out there.

June 22nd ...At the Pilot at the office all day and until 10:50 at night. 16 pages and a original – Philip and I have written on it all the week. Ought to bring results.

This issue of the Pilot contained early Florida history, extolled the virtues of the St. Andrews Bay and its location, and the opportunities in farming, fishing, and more. The paper was George going back to his purpose of promoting the area. St. Andrews needed it even more as the railroad abandonment was made permanent on June 26th. There was no July 4th celebration this year.

July 12th ...Old Jim died this forenoon – Poor old cat – was conscious to the end and wanted to be petted - L buried him in the yard...

August 22nd Nice night – cool – Diary badly neglected – Been out of money for nearly a month – Grace marries Steve Wilson this PM.

August 18th ....write 2 hours and 15 minutes on climatic conditions.

On November 16th Lillian made up the Pilot and ran it herself. George had more frequent days of health issues. But by November 30th, at 77 years old, he felt quite well and was back at the writing. Grace came to the office with a plate of turkey and fruit cake for him. Later that evening George and Lillian went to the Idle Hour.

December 21st ...Philip at linotype – Jones at piston – Lee making up and press – Felix at ads – I write about all day – paper off at 9:45, 14 pages

– lots advertising – a big days work but everything moves off fine shape.

December 24th ...tree is fast being put in shape – B, Mrs. McR, and Mrs. Drummond call in PM. Wait til about 8 for Philip, Maggie, and the boys – out of gasoline on the road. Steve – Grace – Wilbur and Eleanor Rose here 6:30. Had very nice tree – All off by 9 PM. Had several presents – suit of clothes, handkerchiefs, etc.

December 25th ...Receive letters and cards. L and I went to Lynn Haven and visit Philip's new place...

December 27th wind storm from off the Gulf 6 til 8 AM. Blew down some trees...

December 28th ...Got all bills up. Advertising this month $366.70, subscriptions $148.00...

December 31st Very dark all day and at 1 PM there began a very heavy rain that kept up until in the night. High SE wind all day. Felt poorly. Straighten out and check up my bank books – Rained so did not go anywhere today. 1922 ends dark and gloomy as most of the year has been – Am feeling the anxiety and depression of hard times – Have failed in health and gained really in fortune – Had some pleasure in writing.

1923

George worked on finishing his "Old St. Joe" booklet and sent 20 copies to the pharmacy in St. Joe. He and Lillian split the duties, with George writing and printing the Pilot and Lillian handling the St. Andrews Bay News. The linotype was acting up and George had to order replacement parts. Until it was repaired the days at the papers were longer. The couple enjoyed the spelling match at the St. Andrews

Casino and Lillian was becoming quite the sales person, selling more and more of the GCDC lots after years of a poor economy. She handled showing the properties and negotiating the deals. George drew up the deeds.

January 26th ...On getting home at 8 PM find house has been robbed probably since dark this evening as burned matches were scattered all around – my new suit – L's gun, etc. gone – find new shirt and overalls wrapped about 2 bottles soda water on back porch. Find clothes by spring this side fence...look about til 1 – Tracks lead to hill.

Demolition of the tracks to St. Andrews began on February 8th. The trestle over Old Town Bayou (Lake Caroline) was burning, and Mrs. Drummond reported it had been on fire for some time. There was no hope to return rail service to St. Andrews. Literally, the bridge was burned.

But life went on for the Wests. Lillian and George hosted a party on February 16th with 80 people present, and all had a good time. A couple of days later George and Lillian went driving with Grace to Lynn Haven and West End, and then to the Dotys to visit. While at the Dotys, the Drummond house was burned. They managed to save the furniture from the lower story but Drummond lost many valuable papers. The "bad luck" continued around them when Philip's motorcycle was stolen. But spring was on the way and Lillian bought a new dress and hat, and George had some better nights of sleep.

The end of March brought more mishaps as the *Tarpon* tied at the dock caught on fire. The fire did much damage to the main deck mid-ship, but it was saved by the volunteers of the Panama City Fire Department.

Lillian took a brief trip to Birmingham and George drove himself around town for the first time in 9 months. He wrote up the news of the Daughters of the American Revolution having exhumed the remains of Gov. John Clark, his wife, and 2 grandchildren that were near George's house. There was nothing left but some rusted casket handles and nails, and an 1821 Liberty cap dime. The marker, marble slabs, and few artifacts were removed and shipped to Georgia for re-interment.

April 27th Up at 5 – start at 6 for DeFuniak. L takes Mr. Drummond and I to Millville Junction – Kline from there on and back to PC at night – Two hours to Chipley – Nice ride – Swamp at Choctawhatchee something awful – Got to DeFuniak 11:20, 4:45 min – Stopped 15 mins Alford – Meeting not what it should have been – no one there for Jackson County or Calhoun...Start quarter of 5 to get back through the swamp by daylight...Home about 11...

The Kiwanis of Pensacola, previously only interested in promoting Pensacola, had taken on the task of pulling together representatives from across northwest Florida to discuss how they all may collectively promote the area to more settlers. George and Drummond attended the meeting and supported the collective promotion. George and Lillian published the 1922-1923 Pelican, the annual for the Panama High School.

June 21st ...St Clair painted sign...paid $5 cash and to pay 10 in printing. 6 boys 2 girls down to house tonight. L's SS class up til 11:15.

June 28th At Pilot – Long day of it – Make up local page with 4th of July border – Paper off at 9 – As got to PC begins to rain – wind NW. Getting colder. Get wet through – Break windshield trying to close it.

July 30th ...L gets new car...

August 3rd ...*hear early that President Harding died last night..*

August 10th ...*office closed 3 til 4 affairs Harding funeral...*

September 3rd ...*(Leroy) Bare funeral this PM. Masons all out – 12 KKK put in an appearance. First of them showing on public occasion...*

The Alabama Hotel on Harrison Avenue at 3rd Street exploded into flames in the morning of September 6th. The fire destroyed the building and was so hot the windows shattered in the Wilkerson building across Harrison Avenue.

September 10th ...*ordered cutting sticks for paper cutter and two column rules – clouded up in afternoon just after eclipse began – Only saw part of it.*

September 18th ...*L went to Judge Wells funeral. Hot and muggy after rain – Lunar rainbow tonight. Whistling buoy keeps up moaning tonight – never heard it so plain...*

October 4th ...*To PC with L. Philip doping worse. Fell down on street again today – L notifies drug stores to stop selling him narcotics.*

October 13th ...*Find going down to office that fire at 1 AM burned out Mrs. Porter's store at PC and done some damage to Steven's Undertaking parlor – Looks bad – Either robbing or done to put Mrs. P out of business...*

October 15th ...*Stay home about all day and help Hal get in snow peas, clean up jasmine and rose vines on pergola...*

November 25th ...*Gypsies around back yard – drive them off. Go to picture this PM with L.*

November 26th Chickens after fish meal have about destroyed my sweet peas – Stay home all the forenoon and sleep. Do not see why I am so drowsy heart or liver?

December 16th ...Sleep all forenoon – Am to sleepy now days for health – 2 PM and nothing done.

December 20th Up early – at editorial – Pilot. At office working on paper all day. Off at 8 – Post Office 8:15. Stay uptown ¾ hour – Fine 14 page edition Not much editorial.

December 21st ...To office – then to PC. Cannot get bicycle – cannot get anything want – Disappointed...

December 23rd A quiet Sunday. At tree – Got it fixed ...recd lots cards – Get off some...

December 24th Up early and at tree – paper – etc – To PC in PM – Got presents – Rec telegram from W. J. Jackson. Lots cards – Tree at 7:30. Felix – Lee and Peggy came first – Then Grace and children – Warner and Maggie – Philip and Maggie and children – and Lina. Had a grand time. Tree very pretty and everyone lots of presents and happy – to bed at 12....had many presents...

December 28th ...write for Charles' bicycle – also ink

December 31st Fog, 68. Heavy fog all day – worse at night. Cold wave coming – at office all day – wired Chicago Heights Star about yearly meeting notice – fixed up L's application for 1924 license. Get up news editorial and some local. Feel little better tonight. 1923 ends – there has been but little in the years work that has been profitable to me or L. May be worse physically than I was a year ago and may not. Have *more trouble with spells of difficult breathing – no money made and what I took in went out at once*

1924

January 1st   Cloudy, 48 degrees. Chilly day grows colder as day lengthens – not out of the 50's today....checked up bank books – not much to start New Year on – L lost her keys...

January 5th   Starts off at 39 degrees – at noon it was 34 – at 4 PM it was 30 – at 7 it was 26 – 1 degree an hour drop – went over to farm to see about house repairs. Every lock gone and all windows broken... About frozen by 12:30. Gale cuts right through me...

January 6th   Cleared off in night – Kept fire all night in my room but could not get it warm enough to sleep – up at 6 – Temperature 14, water on stove in kitchen froze – also on table in dining room though there was a fire in the fireplace all night. Everything freezable is frozen solid – 30 at noon – 21 at 7 PM

January 7th ...Ella called about fire at Panama – Depot burning. Started up there but out of gas half way up – L went after it. First lot could not get any in engine – Got 5 gals 2nd time and got started – Bad fire no acct of how it happened – Home 11...

The water from the hydrant at 1st Street was insufficient so a fire truck was placed on the dock and water siphoned out of the bay. But the depot and offices of the Atlanta & St. Andrews Bay Railroad Company was destroyed.

Charles' new bicycle arrived and the 12 year old came and stayed with George and Lillian a couple of days. George and Mrs. R. L. McKenzie went to Panama City School and talked on conservation of birds, and using bird houses. The icy cold weather continued, but young Charles braved the cold and rode his bicycle back to the West home.

February 12th   Had rather bad night – up at 6:45 – Got editorial all up – paper ready for press at 4 when grippers would not work. Can't get them to work. Ray Witherill at them from 5 til 9....L's new car broke down. She gets out the old one but that breaks down, or tire off as we try to get home at 9 – A tough day of it all around.

February 13th   ...Fire bells at 3 got us up – looked from here as though it were the printing office. Walk down – Find it to be L. E. Webbs and telephone office – Burned quick....truck down from PC – several roofs caught fire. Press not working yet – no car – L gets her car about 11 –

February 18th   ...Leave Lynn Haven at 9 – Riesota Beach 10:15. 150 in party. 18 states represented – 5 minute speeches – back to Lynn Haven 3:45. 150 fish fried – good time – met Rev. Rooney on street – was Baptist clergyman at Escanaba 1902-09 ...L to PC and gets city printing. Dr. A. L. gets large lot fig cuttings – Hawk over – both early this AM.

Over 136 people travelled on the *Dothan Queen*, the *Clyde*, and the *Dixie III* across North Bay to the winter home of Mr. and Mrs. George J. Ries near the mouth of Cedar Creek. Capt. Lee Youngblood and his brother Clifford provided the transportation by boats, and the fish fry. Guests from each state represented spoke about their home states. George spoke about Florida. But it was Mr. Reis who pointed out though each spoke fondly of their home states, "you all seem to be trying to get away from them and come to Florida". This was the inaugural meeting of the Iowa-Minnesota Society.

Lillian continued selling the GCDC lands, and secured a sale of 10 acres in February. Strawberries were coming in season and she made strawberry shortcake for George at supper.

March 7th ....Woke up at 1:10 AM by Bert who came to tell us they were after us on phone – Nettie's house had burned. L went over and got Mr. Carlisle – L to PC early and gets bolt for press. I did not go to office today – at work on place all day. Put out 30 Cannas – cleared out rose yard – trimmed last of orange trees...

March 14th ...At 5:30 Mrs. Doty called me – wanted me to come up at once – Felix took me up – Webster had died about 5:15...

March 25th ...Go to LH 4:30 PM with L. Klu Klux out on a parade tonight – said to be 35 autos come down to St A....

April 4th ...Felt badly and staid on lounge all forenoon..

April 6th ...to Lynn Haven at 4 – taking George home – picked some wild flowers – calopogous – carnass – Parrot headed Sarracina - Pinguicula – S Flava – Large number flowers out – Ti Ti at it's best. L looked at the horse she bought at auction. Good animal – only paid $15 for it.

April 11th ...Much excitement over the Pilot editorial – Tyler calls on the Klu Klux to take a hand in and go for me...

April 17th ....Old cat has some kittens this AM....Grand jury failed to indict anyone for the rape a 14 year old Millville girl.

April 26th ...Had my picture taken this PM by Masker.

George West, 78 years old, GMW Collection, BCPL

May 13th ...Feel upset over way Baptist Church treating L. Must get up ambition to do something.

George had the job of printing the Pelican annual for Panama High School again.

May 30th Awful hot last night – Did not get to bed until 1 AM. Put on Palm Beach pants this AM. Bought shirt PC this PM – suspenders and ordered Panama hat. To cemetery at 3 and made short address – 50 odd count. L at office tonight completing ballots til midnight.

June 3rd ...heavy vote polled in county – 303 in St. Andrews. Women voting strong – First time – news off 6:30

June 9th ...a very hot night. Took my first bath in tub tonight...

June 15th ...wire for another part of stitcher. Pd telephone bill $2.70...

The stitcher was a machine that did stitch the pages of books together. George's was giving him trouble and he needed a new part for it.

June 16th ...L gets me bathing suit. Put on blue shirt.

June 19th At Pilot all day off at 8:40. Felix – Lee – Peggy and I take it to PC. L has 50 odd boys and girls at the hose tonight.

June 26th Up at 6. L goes to the garage at 7 and finds car gone. Stolen last night. Get out circulars and send out. Notify Lloyd and Gainer. Look up missing men....L gets out old car and using it. Learn convict that has been in employ of Bay Fishery left last night with his clothes. Supposed to be going to Lansing, Mich...

June 27th ...out of breath...Nothing from the car.

June 29th Breeze off Gulf – Feel dull – Hot day – at 5 message came from Chief of Police at Montgomery that he held our car – Called him on phone – It had been left at the Union Station yesterday afternoon. Do not know how it is as to running.

June 30th ...Picked two lotus flowers – gave one to Elmo and one to Gainer

July 4th Up early – at some notes for my speech at Lynn Haven. Start for there at 9:15. Car runs hot. Got in with Dothan boys about halfway there. Speak for 30 mins. Hutchison other speaker. Fine dinner – went up in hydro plane at 3 PM. Unique sights – No particular sensations...To PC with L. Thus ends a busy 4th. Balloting still going on at NY. Saw Phil Maggie and the boys.

The fig trees must have been great in number or size. George and Lillian picked figs by the bushel, and sold many of those. They continued working hard on the papers and other print jobs. Many times with little help.

July 24th ...At proofs all day. Something awful. 30 to 40 lines in a galley...

July 27th ...took first dip of the season in bay...

July 28th ...got car back.

August 5th ...Heavy rain all afternoon. Flooded everything at News (Panama City Publishing Company building).

On August 18th Lillian, Mrs. Burrows, Mrs. Mozley, and Luther set off in her car for a 10 day trip to Montreat, North Carolina. The stopped over in Andersonville, Georgia the first night.

August 21st ....Crawford Adams and folks down tonight to see Mars...sent L Chipley paper has her editorial in it.

Over the next few nights many people came to view Mars through George's telescope including the Bullocks and Steeles.

August 22nd ...came home at 3 and got in tub – 3:30 electrical storm broke – cyclonish. 4 PM took down flag pole. Seemed as though would lift the house – Took down many trees north of here – temp dropped in 15 mins 25 degrees from 99 to 74.

August 27th ...Shark attacks bathers tonight at cement walk. Bit Mrs. Manghum.

About a dozen young people were taking their afternoon swim at the seawall near the Bay Fishery Dock. The shark struck Mrs. Manghum's thigh, but she did not realize she had been bitten. Her husband came in the water to her rescue, and James Gwaltney jumped on the back of the shark, holding it by the dorsal fin. But the shark slipped from his grip and swam away. A few days later when a hurricane was lurking in the Gulf, a shark was spotted by George in the bay in front of his house. Soon several men were there and the shark was killed. It measured over 10' long and was believed to be the shark responsible for attacking Mrs. Manghum.

August 28th ...L gets home at 8 tonight. Was just about going to bed – ate lot grapes and they make me sick...

September 6th ...About 40 girls and boys down here tonight. Take supper on the beach. Stay til 10.

September 7th ...Eleanor Rose down.

200

September 15th Rained heavy about 4 – wind began to increase and changed to NE...reports hurricane moving north - at 7 begins to blow with hurricane force NE by N – At 8 limbs begin to go and tops of some trees – 9 is at its worst 100 miles an hour...chimney of kitchen blew off – pergola went down about 9:30 – window in lavatory blew in – cedars are worst damaged – Lets up by 10:30 – but keeps up gusts all day. L sold lot $55 cash. Shark killed at 2 PM in front of house.

September 16th Cool north wind holds on – Result of hurricane begins to show up... Trees down everywhere – roads blocked – much damage all about us. To PC 5. Bunch trees blown down at ?? – Boys fixed up old engine and ran off half News. No lights. Had to quit at 5:15. No lights or power today. No news from eastward yet.

Once in the Gulf of Mexico the path of this 1924 hurricane was relatively similar to the path of Hurricane Michael in 2018. George was able to secure help quickly from John Surber who rebuilt the chimney just 2 days after the hurricane.

September 27th ...Grace has daughter born about 3 this AM. My sixth great grand child. Went in and saw it at 5:30 – A large child ...

This was Betty Jean Wilson, born to Grace and Steve.

October 4th ...saw Dr. Blackshear – He prescribes 30 grain strychnine for me 2 or 3 times a day. Get it. Take tablet tonight...

October 5th ...Feel little better...

October 6th S wind – warmer – Feel poorly – Pulse but 28 – write for both papers...

October 18th ...Eleanor Rose had tonsils and adenoids out at Club House.

October 19th ...Mrs. Vancleve (from) Lynn Haven calls on phone and asks if I will give 15 min talk on Nov 14th before Lynn Haven Literary Club on Spanish Occupation of Florida. Agree to do so. To PC 5 – Call on Grace – baby doing well.

George hired Quilla Barnes and Charles Knowles who came and helped George clean up the debris from the hurricane and get the pergola back up.

On October 24th the Bay Harbor dock of St. Andrews Bay Lumber Company was ablaze, and also the ship *Valdarno* and 2 barges, all loaded with lumber. George praised the work of the Panama City Fire Department for getting the fire extinguished, restricting the damage to the dock, which was a total loss. The barges broke loose and floated into the bay. The Fire Department drenched the lumber on the dock trying to save it. Over 1 million board feet of lumber was estimated to be lost.

October 27th ...Grace had Betty Jean down at 5 in auto first ride out.

October 29th ...Sen. Fletcher is on Tarpon – Sherman was there to meet him and took him to Millville. Went to PC. Shaved and haircut – 10:30 met Fletcher – He comes to St. Andrews at 1:30 with R. L. McKenzie – we go to school house then to PC School - 4:30 return to office...

Duncan Fletcher had served as Mayor of Jacksonville and rebuilt it after the Great Fire of 1901. He later served as president of the Gulf Inland Waterways Association, and was elected to the United States Senate in 1909 and served 5 terms. There he served on committees including the one to investigate the *Titanic* disaster, and the Banking and Currency Committee that investigated the cause of the Wall Street crash of 1929. His committee known as the Pecora Commission reformed banking with the passage of the Securities Act of 1933 and the Securities Exchange Act of 1934. In 1928 Fletcher introduced the legislation that created the Everglades National Park which was signed into law by President Franklin D. Roosevelt in 1934.

November 7th ...Doty and wife at office and we settle the Webster Doty claim by giving A. Duane Doty deed to the 40 acre farm tract – So ends what was to have been a gift to me by Col. Doty and Webster of $1,500 in aid of putting in a first class printing plant at St A and for other work legal and otherwise done for Webster – A clear loss to me of $2,500...

The 40 acre farm tract was adjacent to Oakland Cemetery, where for years George grew cabbage, sweet potatoes, and other crops in season.

November 27th ...Thanksgiving day...to movies tonight PC "Covered Wagons" very good – home late....

November 28th ...Slept til 7 – 79th birthday...

December 7th ....Cleaned out the pool and found the gold fish...hear tonight of council selling out to PC on cement walk – spite work against Drummond.

December 19th ...largest paper ever got out...worked at map and picture for advertising.

The December 19th Panama City Pilot was the largest. There were 20 pages and many advertisements. George and Lillian were busier than ever, and Zelina "Lina" Brown wrote to a relative named Lillie about them. Lillie was intending to come to St. Andrews and visit. Lina took on the task of explaining to Lillie there was no room for her to stay. Lina wrote that she had no room, Grace and Steve only had one room and her 9 year old daughter Eleanor Rose slept in the room with them, and that Philip and Maggie had only a small house for them and the 4 boys.

"George and Lillian have a room but as she has no time for house-keeping and seldom has a servant, takes advantage of any woman coming to the house, to get her to act as cook and housekeeper. They are busy business people, who are at home only to eat hurried meals and sleep. If dinner is ready at twelve or one o'clock they probably walk in about three. Seven-thirty or eight they may arrive for supper..."

December 22nd ...Tree came today and we got it up this evening and L got it trimmed and most of presents on.

December 24th Cloudy, 34 degrees. Growing colder – L finishes tree – work only half a day in office – Maggie and boys come 6:30 Grace and two girls....I am short breath – not well all day. To PC. Philip did not come to tree...all had many presents...

December 31st Cloudy, 52 degrees. Warmer – SW wind. At Pilot – Got editorial ready this PM. Feel very poorly. No appetite...1924 drawn to a close – Health faded me this year – stomach and heart – Financially we are doing better as year closes – Plenty of work in office and paying rate but short of good help.

1925

George's handwriting in the diaries of the 1920's is more and more difficult to read, with 1925 becoming more so. He had a variety of symptoms and ailments and started the year seeing Dr. Blackshear. George took cod liver oil, yeast cakes, put hot water on his eye that was terribly bloodshot, and Dr. Blackshear removed a mass from his ear. Breathing was painful, he was short of breath often, and his ribs near his heart were sore sometimes. He wrote from home more often rather than going to the office in St. Andrews or Panama City. Stomach and heart issues came and went randomly with no warning. These last 2 years of his life are best presented by his own diary entries.

January 12th Work 4 hours on the address I am to deliver this PM at the Lynn Haven Chautauqua. Finish it at 1 PM. L takes Drummond and I up – Feel fairly well – Good audience – Home by 6.

January 23rd Feel some better – up 7:40. Clean up papers at 12:15 sat down at the typewriter to write Hayes at Pensacola Journal – Had finished it but last line – when next I knew I found myself on the floor in front of machine (the typewriter) and fireplace. Heat of fire felt on my face – Do not know how long I had been there – possibly 10 minutes – perhaps not as long – Had no feeling of dropping off or coming to or while was unconscious – Called Ella & L came in soon – while standing by table 1:15 went down again – Philip here by 5:30. About 7 I had another spell. L called Dr. Blackshear here PM.

January 24th Went to bed at 4 yesterday PM and been there since...Quite a few in – Dr. Blackshear down – Grace, Betty Jean...and Maggie down.

January 25th Poor night. Head feels bad – working it all night – I construct sentences – articles – and rearrange til I am tired out. Zada brought in a nice lunch – In PM Mrs. Holliday brought in fine strawberries and whipped cream – Grace Drummond – J. H. Drummond and Lina in – Mary Moore in late – Brought me some camellias.

January 26th Feel poorly this AM. Rather bad night. Felix brought me some fine grapefruit. Mary brought some custard...A long day. L to St. Andrews this AM. No one in this PM. Philip staid last night. Went through papers today.

January 28th Slept better – Dictate to L editorial for Pilot...feeling better – But can go but about 4 hours without taking something into my stomach – food or medicine – Arms ache.

January 29th Write some for Pilot. Feeling little better – read Pilot proof brought down by Stokes – L brought Dr. Blackshear down at noon.

February 1st Cold this morning – up late. Ella notified us this noon that she was quitting – Is going to move today to her house at panama – Lee and Peggy call – Felix calls – Get up this noon and get dressed and down stairs – First time since last week Friday – Stay down til 7:30 – Feel fairly well...call up Grace....Wrote all News editorial this evening – dictate to L. Auto tag came today.

Someone often stayed with George during these days. Lillian was running the papers and GCDC sales of lots for homes, businesses, agricultural land, and 50' by Tarpon Dock. She showed property and figured the receipts for sales. Real estate continued to boom as it had in 1924.

February 6th ...down to office couple hours in PM...

February 7th ....dinner downstairs...The gang howling over the Pilots lots...

February 13th ...have box of candy L brings home tonight – 16th wedding anniversary...

February 28th ....Little "Baby Cat" dies this AM. Tried to get in my room in the night – To PC tonight with L when she took Frank – Edith – and Ella up there. Saw Mattie Dixon this evening – She is looking better than I ever saw her.

March 12th Dense fog all night. Warm. Slept very well until 6 – Bad 6 til 8. Better by noon. Letter from Jackson – Philip came down – is at tax reduction matter...Dr. Whitfield here at 5 and looked me over...

George's ailments continued and he had a suffocating feeling in his chest. He began to read much about his trouble, and though he never wrote a specific diagnosis in his diary, congestive heart failure could possibly be one of many problems he was experiencing. Some diary entries sound like he also had a hernia. He did write in 1926 that he had eczema. In the spring he looked over the Satsuma groves and called them "fine". The train from Dothan brought visitors to Panama City regularly and the springtime numbers were 75 or more on the train each time.

March 27th ....George and Charles over this PM. George stays.

April 19th Warm – not feeling well. Mr. Carlisle came this morning – George home at 2 PM. L to Millville this PM to get her father's things. Rode down to Post Office at 5 – Feel bad – Nothing appears to stop trouble in my stomach – Received extension GCDC charter today – quick work. Mr. and Mrs. W. L. Wilson here awhile this forenoon – he is after L's Callaway property...old cat has 3 kittens last night in library wood box. Cora home this PM.

Cora Bess had come to work for the Wests at the house and moved her family there.

April 21st Rested well last night – wrote News editorial – To office PM and read proof – L brings home Airedale puppy...

April 24th ...Charles down this PM for weekend – feel quite well today til 5 PM.

April 30th Cold spell. 57 degrees this morning. Had to have fires. Used up again – Think cold does it. To office all forenoon. Recd proof – write some. Smith finished plowing 3:25 awful job. At home in PM. About 4 began to be troubled for health – Kept it up all evening – did not sleep – L to PC and office 2 or 3 times – paper not off until nearly 12 – Lost little time by fuse burning out – Big paper – 12 pages – tax list.

May 5th Slept very well – but begin to feel bad by noon – dr. Whitfield called this PM. Decides on change medicine – Take Nux Vomica and Hydrastas – to PC and get it...

Hydrastas was derived from a plant and used to treat a variety of ailments including ulcers, digestive problems, and as a diuretic. Vomica Nux was derived from the Strychnine tree and used for treatment of digestive diseases, heart and circulatory system disorders.

May 6th Warm day – had a very bad night. Slept but little. Sat in chair most of night. To office this AM then to PC. Saw Philip...

May 8th Feel poorly – Done too much and too much worry yesterday. Fire in street end on my lot used up about all my wild garden – Damage to us over $500.

May 9th bad night and day...To office this AM and PM but can hardly breathe at times – L gets offer for Callaway property $75 per acre but Stokes tries to quell the deal – men cutting out Baker Street yet.

May 10th ..Mother's day – pick some pretty pink and red roses to place by mother's picture.

May 19th ...To office and finish News editorial – Begin to feel poorly by noon. L rubs me after dinner. Feel little better – slept very well last night...

May 21st Up early. Down to office write remainder editorial for Pilot – read proofs etc. Said that Keith sells Bunker Cover property $1,000 an acre 600 acres. We sold him 80 acres of it close in for $50 an acre – All excitement over sales.

May 24th Rain from 4 til 5 AM. Lay abed late. Change to Palm Beach pants today. Wash my head – ride little in PM.

May 25th ...L's car in shop this PM.

May 30th ...car acting queer tonight. L takes in over $1,000 today GCDC & PC.

June 1st To office then to PC early – stay til noon and back again in PM. Talk with many – A new leadership asserting itself in PC. The Sudduth and other outside parties are planning on running the town – The old regime is passed.

June 7th ...Aunt Anna failing fast

June 10th ...Aunt Anna died about 2:30 this afternoon. Feel too bad to get up there ...

June 11th ...L has all arrangements made for funeral Aunt Anna – Laura down – She goes with L tomorrow. Gave L $7 – Had first water meter at office this PM.

June 12th Clear at 4 when we got up – getting ready for L and George to go to Marianna to Aunt Anna's funeral – off at 6:15...back at 6:30 tonight...

June 19th Hot – Philip down this AM and I dictate several letters connected with dividend 15 – Sent out all checks I have received account of the stock held...

This was the 15th dividend paid to GCDC stockholders that were confirmed as owning stock and the number of shares.

June 20th Hot night. Try to straighten out my desk affairs this AM. Badly mixed up on numbers – Deposit my dividend check – endorse L's and Philip's note for $525 half of what Philip puts in his abstract business...

June 29th ...Grace – Eleanor Rose – and Betty Jean in this PM. Went to PC 4:30 Saw the Photostat machine start working and Philip made his first pictures – or copies of maps etc – A fine machine...

July 2nd ...Middleton delivered 760 ft rough lumber for walks and fence...

July 3rd ...listened to Greb-Walker Fight at NY.

July 4th Hot and humid – Quiet day – nothing doing. Not even a flag up anywhere. No patriotism shown...Linotype agent and Felix down early. L signed up for a model 14 – about $5,000

The model 14 was the Mergenthaler Linotype George and Lillian purchased for the publishing building in St. Andrews.

July 7th A bad day for me. Worry all day. All kinds of troubles coming up – First Miller and Brice not making good – Threaten to tie up our property...notify them we will end contract – Miss Lockey states there is an old judgement on record against GCDC...Painter in our absence puts coat nasty yellow on house...

July 10th Hot as ever – up to 90 every day. Men finished walk to back gate, hung gate – fixed windows upstairs, door to gas house – etc. Painter on front ...

July 13th ...3 lot people here for figs today...

July 16th ...Ella brought over the cows – No one here at work today. Cora put up figs...

July 20th ...Charles down – picks figs...Head feels bad by noon – L makes out 3 deeds.

July 21st Dozed all day I think – No recollect of time today – Breathing difficult. Dr. J comes at 11. Had vomited some yellow bile – Dr gave some medicine that began to take effect about 6. In bed all day when began to wake up at 5:30 PM thought it was morning and could not believe it was night – could not raise up today without help. Legs appeared to be weak and had no power to straighten up...

July 24th Rec $40 from Hollywood magazine for "Yuccas" article.

July 25th ...L's car not working ...Philip and Maggie drive down tonight. Take Charles home with them....

July 27th ...Fuse blew out tonight as we go to bed – 45 mins getting it fixed – no air – no lights

July 30th ...Quiet day but am sick and I realize it.

July 31ˢᵗ Hot as ever. Did not put on my clothes today...July has been the worst month I ever experienced in Florida – Nearly every day above 90...

August 1ˢᵗ ...Mr. Carlisle went to Nettie's this PM. Quieter in the house...

August 2ⁿᵈ 72 degrees, cool morning – Slept until 7:30. Shave – up late – keep quiet – must write some but have no ambition. L and D to church – 90 by noon. Fingers shaky.

August 13ᵗʰ ...Stay alone part of forenoon...Dr Ward and Whitfield here at noon – Ward gave me an examination all over...

August 14ᵗʰ Slept very well – hot night and forenoon...Down stairs in night shirt most of forenoon..

August 15ᵗʰ ....Col. Page and Bullock crowd call for a Boosters meeting Monday night. They are bound to finish up St. Andrews.

August 20ᵗʰ ...Did not sleep much. Up at 3...down to office at 9 – stay til 12:10. Felix brings me home...Good breeze at the office – none in the house....got my medicine tonight that drs ward and whitfield prescribed. To bed 11 – sat out on porch an hour...

August 22ⁿᵈ ...Ed Masker here again to photo pear tree...

August 26ᵗʰ ...Take ride in Payne's new $4,600 Cadillac

A. A. Payne was one of the owners of the Panama Hotel and purchased his new car from partner F. M. Nelson owner of the Buick agency in Panama City.

August 30ᵗʰ Philip here before I got downstairs...Mr. Carlisle, Nettie, and Pitt down – L's B day. Decide to make dividend and loan Lillian

$1,000 to pay on linotype.

September 2nd Philip down at 6:30. Sees Hutchison and Sapp – Latter here at 8:45. Miller and Snow here 9 – Go over contract. I hold to my reply to them of July 7th. Coming from office at 11 – Harries, Snow, and Miller meet us at Pratt garage corner and tender me first payment on contract which expired month or more ago...

September 7th ...Sent Will $2,000 being balance due on the principal of mortgage note on the house.

October 1st ...Poole here at noon to set up the linotype.

October 3rd ...Poole finished putting up linotype and cast first line. Williams set up all faces we have on both machines...

October 4th ...Marion Bay and George down – Philip getting tired out with worries.

October 5th ...To office at 8 – The 14 running all right. To PC for dinner at Cook's...wrote National Insurance Co – also copy dept of patent office about word Realtor.

October 8th A very hot night last night. L used up this AM. Too much to do – papers off at 6 – good work.

October 16th ...Do not like look of things real estate....Took typewriter to Coe Wallace and he fixed it at once.

October 18th ...Letter from Jackson upsets me – Philip down we do some work on abstract...down at night – brings Charles back.

October 21st ...Ebba and Horace give me set of the Govt naval reports of Civil war that belonged to Lieut Colonel or Commander Shephard.

October 23rd ...write hurricane Island story – Stay home in AM. Little black dog died last night. To PC evening – feel discouraged..

October 27th ...at office all day – clean up some – did not go to PC today.

October 29th ...did not go to PC. Head has been dizzy today – Bad feeling in my chest..

November 11th ..To school at 11:15 and address children 35 minutes on Armistice Day...

November 12th ...To PC late. Saw many – Pilots in demand.

November 14th ...Esop A Martin name of darky at work on yard – work with him this forenoon at old fig tree – Get it up all right. Did not go to PC today – at office in PM...

November 18th ...Pay Martin 7.50 3 days work...He goes tomorrow for his wife.

November 20th ...at office most of day – To PC later in PM – Stokes wires Russ (the) bill consolidating Millville – PC – and St Andrews passed this PM. Another outrage on the...Boys and girls down tonight from St. Andrews to look through telescope.

This was the legislative bill for consolidation of the towns, which George and Lillian had been against for many years. The bill was signed by the Governor on this day and the consolidation would be effective March 12th, 1926.

November 21st ...much excitement over the consolidation of cities.

November 22nd ...Can not sleep – Do not know what to do – Matters get worse – Read a great deal to get foundation for this weeks papers...

November 23rd ...Up late at office – Not much doing – Everyone disgusted over the consolidation work.

November 25th Up early – to office all at work – L buys turkey – Charles went home tonight – Did not know when he was – paper off at 11:45 a day ahead of time...

November 26th Clear – up at 7:15 and built fires – fed chickens – maple coffee and oatmeal – feel very well. A nice warm morning...

November 29th Nothing doing – quiet day – Mr. Carlisle came to stay – Nettie had turned him out. L goes to quarters and hires a woman called Annie. Philip leaves some trout they caught today.

November 30th L has bad cold but is out all day – To office early – write W. J. Jackson and Seneff – Sent dividend checks – Anna here – Esop Martin back – works today.

December 1st up late. L in bad way – lungs pain her. Call Dr. Zediker 11 – at office most of day – Philip down early to look up tax receipts 1915. Find them – City trying to collect again. Sent out last of dividend checks – Martin works today – Elliott brings me down and back. Man at typewriters. Did not get "P" fixed tonight on the office machine.

December 2nd L up this AM. Not feeling well. L in bad shape but much better that yesterday...

December 3rd ...No. 14 broke down – off 10 PM at office 10:30. Home 11:10. Disgusted with matters – Martin worked half day... Pd him 8.75. L's cold is much better...

December 5th 44, cloudy, cold, chilly SW wind – To office AM. Get off some mail Pd Annie this noon $6 one week tomorrow night – Sent to E.

C. Robbins Ashford, NC for Christmas tree and two boxes greenery for Blanch S and Blanche McR...

December 6th ..Up 7:30 Feel very well – Cold in house – Looked over many papers – Did not write any – Cold day – Charles not coming down til morning. Talk some with Drummond – He wants to leave here.

December 9th ...at office – Met Capt Barrow – to boat with him – write all day – Elliott went to B-T. They try to get all our men. Notified to look out for myself...

Elliott was an employee at either the St. Andrews Bay News or Pilot, and the B-T was the Beacon Tribune published by Sherman's men. Keeping workers at a printing company was a challenge, as George had frequently written in his diary. The competition for sober employees was fierce.

December 10th Up 7:30 Legs very painful. Cold weather – paper off late but a good paper and short of help too.

December 16th ...Will Hatten came at 2:30 Looks well. Talk some with him on business matters...

December 19th ...Will Look and R. L. McKenzie down at 9 – Got at settlement with Hatten – He agrees to take $11,500 with the about $500 he has had – Will and McKenzie turn over $2,000 note each their payment. I am to pay $533 cash and note for $3,300 six months – take up old note of $10,000 – Our 1/3's are $3,833 each...

George, Lillian, and the Gulf Coast Development Company were struggling financially. The news papers never were profitable, and it was not George's intention to make money from the papers, but to promote St. Andrews Bay. Everyone involved in the Bank of Panama

City had to put in money after the embezzlement in 1915. This was the final settlement of that old debt.

December 23rd   Pilot 30 pages

December 24th 32 degrees, clear, warming up since midnight. Legs bad – very painful – Go to office – get checks made out for L $225, Philip $20, Grace $15, Maggie $10, George $5 – Tree finest ever – L gets everything on early – Pilot mailed this AM day ahead of time. Maggie and Warren, Lina, Grace, Eleanor Rose, Betty Jean, and Wilbur and girl and Philip, Maggie, and the 4 boys and Mr. Carlisle and Annie at tree – Through by 9.

December 27th 36 degrees, clear, N wind – getting very cold at night – Fear for trees.

December 28th clear, 18 degrees, very cold – N winds cut down all tender vegetation. Do not know about orange trees – Our pipes froze up and burst. Bad shape.

December 29th ...sent Mergenthaler Company two checks $342 on linotype...

1926

January 1st 32 degrees, cloudy. Up late as did not get to bed til 12 – warmer – Tony here and at work at books cleaning. Awful shape. No money coming in and none in bank. Big party last night at the Sherman Apts. Itching terribly today. Philip sold his two lots $3,200...

January 2nd Tony and I at the library – look for Dr. Ward to call... Warren – Maggie – Grace and Betty Jean call...Tony 3 days work $5 – Rec $5 for rent – Two men from Hicks here to fix pipes – Got part of them fixed.

George had rented a small house on his property for $5 a month to John Powell. That was the $5 rent money he collected the next few months.

January 3rd 50 degrees, Rainy. Up early and go to see Dr. Ward who goes on the morning train – Says my trouble is squamous eczema – Gives me prescriptions – To Danfords and get groceries...

January 4th 58 degrees, cloudy. Feel better – To PC early and there til noon and again in PM. First time have spent day there in a long time. Not much doing at office in AM and at bank.

January 5th 61 degrees, Rain. Very heavy rain from midnight on – Runs down chimney – L gets new Chevrolet today – Engine no. is 2146797. Tag no. 215880.

January 6th ...Looked up my trip with Ringling Brothers Circus in 1899 on my train. L and Charles to PC tonight to show – Home 9:45. Sat up and talked with Dale about old times. L gets auto license today – No. 215880.

January 7th ...As wait at office for paper began Ringling article – wrote 2 hours on it.

January 8th 43, cloudy. Raw cloudy day. Had fearful time last night itching – Drove me wild – Heart almost stopped beating. Stay home today looking up data for writing.

January 10th ...wrote several editorials for the Pilot and the Ringling Brothers article.

January 11th ...L let Elliott go this PM.

January 12th To office early – Elliott, probably, had put nasty oil in magazine.

January 14th ...St. Andrews grants electric light franchise tonight – No one knew of it...

By January 16th, through Lillian collecting payments owed, the No. 14 linotype was paid for in full.

January 19th ...To office early – There about all day. Bad time last night. Palpitations heart – worried over suits etc – Quiet day – visited Seberts Stoneworks.

January 20th Cool – Feel better slept well – not up last night – first night in months have slept so – Big whiskey haul at Manghums last night – have big weeks work ahead...

January 21st clear, mild day – to office all day – much to do – Many callers...Parker down and get facts of his life – Jones men in – Fine show of narcissus these days.

January 23rd Clear, cold. Icycles at garage this AM...

January 27th ...Sent Florida Historical Society $2 dues.

January 29th Misting most of day – rain at 5 – up very late – 9 – Do not feel well today – Head dizzy chest upset – at office til 1

January 30th ...Pd Annie, Grace called – Got at cleaning up of the closet..

January 31st ...Looking over things in closet. Do not feel well...

February 2nd Rain in PM. Charles out in auto smash..

February 7th ...L at library today and I help get it in very good shape by 4 – feel poorly – short of breath head dizzy...

February 11th ...Heart very irregular – slow – Head feels bad. Have a cold – not up til 9

February 17th At Pilot – Do not feel like writing. Many crooked things coming up at PC. We no longer have any voice in matters there. At PC ordered pane glass for office – Charles has bead rising on his lip. Dr. Zediker opened it – New bank to be started at PC. Stokes et al.

February 20th ...looked over old diaries – L and Charles to Lynn Haven this PM.

February 28th Mr. Carlisle worse – L calls Dr. B for him. Annie not here today...

March 7th ...Short of breath or difficult to breathe.

March 9th ...Election day – To PC and voted 2 PM – There again at 6 – Someone stealing our wood last two nights. Think it people in Foxworth place. Large number of High School girls and boys down to look through telescope.

From the March 9th, 1926 St. Andrews Bay News:

Hail Caesar, those who are about to die salute you

St. Andrews has fallen. That honored and loved title, the name of one of Christ's much beloved disciples, has been torn down from the proud eminence it has occupied for a hundred years, to gratify personal spite; to enrich those who would, through the act of supine legislature, and the approval of a pliant governor, attach and tax widely separated sections of this bay country, to pay an indebtedness brought about by graft and profiteering, and to control a people with which the despoilers have no sympathy, no business connection, and nothing in common. In fact, it brings taxation to a large portion of this city without representation. This is one of the most unconstitutional features of the Annihilation Act.

With but one voice out of five in the new city government, but with about one half its territory, our people will not have any power in the council of the new city, no power to secure needed legislation, to even lay a sidewalk, pave a street, build a bridge, obtain city water or fire protection. They control our police, if we have any given us by this antagonistic body of lawmakers. We will be taxed heavily to maintain an expensive staff of officials whose only business will be to carry on political agitation, and to retain in office our oppressors.

"O mighty Caesar! Dost thou lie so low? Are all thy conquests, glories, triumphs, spoils, shrunk to this little measure?"

For nearly four hundred years St. Andrews has held a prominent place on the north gulf coast. Discovered by one of the early Spanish navigators of the Mexico Gulf, a Saint's name was given it, which, when this section came into the possession of the United States, was given the settlement here, and ever since it has been known by the name of St. Andrews. But as the poet has said, "Death loves a shining mark, a signal blow," and within the past few years there has arisen in this region "A new king over Egypt, which knew not Joseph," and the mandate went forth to despoil and destroy those who inhabited the land. And thoroughly has this command been carried out so far as the city of St. Andrews is concerned. But "Assassination makes only martyrs, not converts," and the martyrdom of St. Andrews may possibly result as did the martyrdom of the disciple at Achia. But many who have known St. Andrews from their childhood up; who have sported upon its beaches; who have fished in its waters; who have rejoiced in outings spent here, will regret the despoilation which has taken away its hundred year old name, and they will curse those accountable therefor. Sadly say Farewell! The sea is calling tonight, and with its call St. Andrews slips its leash, and passes out across the bar. Farewell! A long Farewell.

The consolidation was completed and after this ran in the paper, many people locally and from afar commended the writing. George then wrote *"...the almighty dollar is too powerful for sentiment, reason, or the democratic rights of a citizenship."*

March 14th 27 degrees, 26...Freezing water pipes in kitchen and up stairs frozen up. Awful night.

March 18th clear, north wind - very cold last night. Had a bad nightmare. At office 9 til 1 – writing for Pilot....have 18 (employees) connected with printing plant today...

March 20th ...at office at 9. At the Lynn Haven Free Press – Named it after my Ripon Free Press of 1871-73. Off at 2:30. Good looking 8 page paper D. C. Sawyer Lynn Haven manager. Took them to Lynn Haven. Three papers now to handle ...heart hurts again 3 PM on.

March 21st Mild. First spring day we have had. Felt bad 2 til 8 – stay home all day...Short of health from 4 on...

March 22nd ...Bad time with my heart 4 til 7 – Do not feel at all well. Annie about used up (with a) cold – Charles brought 2 nice bass...

March 23rd ...Annie worse – Feel poorly after 4:30. Got Lee carpenter to work for us today – Fix floor and back door and walk at Panama City

Pilot. Went to PC 2 and got some wire screen for front verandah – Lee worked til 5.

March 27th …bargain this evening for 2-hand whit-lock 7 – column press $2800

March 29th …Sign up for a whitlock press this PM. 3 weeks delivery…

April 5th …set up til 10:20 waiting for L to come. L got new stove this PM. Small one – Men put it up. Powell pays rent $5.

April 6th 56, clear. Nice morning. Carpenters here this AM to put shingles on kitchen roof. Annie back this AM Sick yesterday – 3 men at work all day.

April 8th …Pay carpenters 34.50 for shingling kitchen roof.

April 10th …Mr. Carlisle wants to go to Dothan have cancer treatment.

April 14th …Mr. Thompson died about 3 this AM….feel poorly this evening – Do not know why.

April 24th …At night go down and look at Radio that L wants put in.

April 26th …Radio put in today – 12:30 first voice comes in from Mobile – New Orleans & c.

April 30th …Smith and I clearing – Pay him tonight 5 days work at $3 per day - $15. Have got much clearing done. L and Charles to Callaway this PM to see how much live oak Bay Fisheries had stolen – find 10 trees (have been cut). *Posted her land.*

May 4th ...at office in forenoon – Disgusted with the way work is carried on – wrote article 5 PM to 7 PM for Pilot. Powell pays $10 for two months rent.

May 6th 60 degrees, clear. Up and dressed by 7. At once was taken with pain in my chest and abdomen – breath cut off – and could not breathe – called Whitfield and Zediker. Took 2 tablets...and nitroglycerine before they got here – Zediker gave me hypodermic of morphine and other medicines – at 8 AM Grace and Philip here – Began to let up – an awful attack – could not stand 15 mins more of it...

May 7th Feel very poorly. Took another pill cascara in night and salts this AM...Feel some better by 5. To PC 6 – Last evening Zada brought me some ice cream Mrs. Holliday some gladiolas and Mrs. Johnson and Surber some roses.

May 8th ...Slept little better – Feel it – Heart irregular...

May 12th ...talk today of putting R. L. McKenzie in as City Manager.

May 19th ...Paid Miley 9.45, 3 weeks milk bill – To PC PM. See Philip...George comes down.

May 21st ...Got up RR article...

May 23rd ...Philip – Maggie and the children down at night – Rode about some this PM.

George knew his days were getting short and began to take care of business to make things simpler at his passing.

May 24th ...Philip down this AM and I make over to him the 10 acres in Sec 5 north of the cemetery. To office 9 – George starts 2 weeks schooling at PC.

May 26th ...Finish papers today making homeplace over to L. Mrs. Singletary of Millville brought me some fine hydrangeas.

May 27th ...Mrs. Holliday sent me jar of May Haw jelly. First I ever tasted.

May 31st ...Memorial day. Took no part in it. Not well enough...

June 1st 73 degrees, clear. Bad time 4 to 6:30, up at 9 – at office – Read proof early – Quiet day Nothing doing. To PC with Felix 5:30 and with L at 7:30. Saw Dr. Adams – Did not know him from Crawford. Radio working good tonight.

June 10th ...Up 7:30 but up every hour or so since 1:20. Was then taken with a heart attack – beat rapidly – took bisodol...and a spoonful ammonia – and belladonna - Call Zediker but am over worst of it when he comes...

June 14th ...at office...not so well.

June 18th ...work on my bank affairs all day. Tires me. Cannot get it to agree with bank – Cannot locate the about $50 that the bank credits me more than I can make out on my book.

June 29th ..68 degrees, clear. Cool night – Slept well until 2:30 up and down at 7. Worried about money matters – Do not feel good all day – To PC at night. No one comes to see me – No one wants to meet Mr. Carlisle who is always on front porch.

July 2nd ...A very hot night – slept under the big fan. Shave – change pants – get up to PC 10:15. L has car decorated – Get in procession – mixed up affair. Had bad time with my stomach 4 til 8. Got some carbonated water at PC. Helps it – Up at 8 and see fireworks – a good display.

July 3rd ...Busy at office getting in boxes & c. new press...No cement after 9 til 12...find L on road. She gets $1,000 today....looks favorable raising money for press $2650...Phil down today. Bay and Phil home with Philip.

July 5th ...someone around house at 3 AM....

July 6th ...Feel very shaky this AM. Not over it til 9 ...L picks first figs.

July 8th ...Dodson man came to put up press this AM. Got boys helping. Good days work...

July 10th ...Not well this Forenoon. To the office to see the press start – Pulley too large – got it going 5 PM...L got in the amount necessary to pay for the press and expenses – a big days work.

July 12th ...Mr. Carlisle left this AM for Millville.

July 17th ...Pd light company $4 – Telephone $2.40 – Annie $6...

July 31st 81 degrees, clear. A very hot night but strong wind off the Gulf. At office and read proof – Free Press off at 1:30. In PM went to Bayou George... Found some new flowers to me – Also saw some yellow orchids – Home at 8 – To PC with figs at 9 AM...

Steve and Grace, Courtesy Wilson Funeral Home

August 1ˢᵗ ...Steve (Wilson, Grace's husband) and Betty Jean call – To school house hill where two autos collided this PM...felt poorly all day.

August 4ᵗʰ 74 degrees, clear. Bad time from 3 til 8 – stomach and coughing... A dull day and am discouraged – Outlook poor.

August 5ᵗʰ ...L gets place in Mrs. Truesdell's office for Pilot office at Lynn Haven...

August 13ᵗʰ ...Feel poorly all day. Friday and the 13ᵗʰ – Bad combination...

August 16ᵗʰ ...Fowler – T – and Reese all drunk this afternoon – Reese worked this forenoon only. ...says B-T (Beacon-Tribune) has 5 to 10 gal liquor on hand all time. There's where Fowler got his this AM...

Fowler, "T", and Reese were all employees at George and Lillian's news papers.

August 17ᵗʰ ...Fowler and his boys still on drunk...

August 23ʳᵈ George came down with Charles...

August 26ᵗʰ ...tide high – Nothing from the storm – At office at Pilot all day and til 11:10 at night – Got it in Post Office 11:30 PM. 2 sections – 24 pages – about 100 ads – Big paper – Run part off on new press – works very well. High seas on the Gulf.

Panama City had started efforts to purchase property across from the Sherman Hotel, which many believed would be strictly for the hotel and George took up this one last cause. He wrote that the hotel owners knew they needed more land to provide a setting for the building but had neglected to purchase the additional property. The price on the proposed park acreage had most recently been $40,000, but when the

City talked of buying it, the price jumped to $47,000. GCDC had given land for parks in Panama City and George believed there should be parks of all sizes and on the beach front along the bay for all to enjoy. He believed it was the City's responsibility to plan for and provide parks, and that any proposed subdivisions should be required to provide parks.

September 8th ...feel poorly – Too much trouble – Gang trying to steal our property – Fowler going to knife Felix today – I take a hand in and put Fowler on his side of the shop – L late to supper again – About 7:30 when I get away from the office.

September 13th ...Charles begins school this AM

September 17th ...Council bought the park...

September 20th Hurricane here in full force – Rain driven in sheets – Lines all down – went to office at noon. No one out – no school – wind still south. Blows in puffs up to 75 miles an hour I think – center storm W-SW of us – Probably will strike land today Pensacola or near there. Tide up...about 3 ft above normal here – marshes filled with birds – about 7 inches rain fell today.

September 21st ...everyone at repairs – no current (electricity) til 7 this evening...all kinds of rumors as to loss of life and property at Pensacola and Mobile – Nothing serious here.

September 24th...very hard to breathe...

September 30th ...Mr. Carlisle went to PC this AM and did not come back until after 6 PM. L could not find him – made 2 trips to do so – Hired man to bring him home.

Lillian had a sick father, a sick husband, and was running all the businesses.

October 3rd ...David Smith called and I arranged to have him work a little this week...

October 4th ...Dave Smith here 7 AM at work

October 5th David Smith at the place in garden, am going to put out bulbs.

October 6th ...show David S about putting in bulbs...No. 14 broke down.

October 14th 68 degrees, clear. Cool night. Up every hour – In bad shape this AM.

October 15th ...Ebba here this PM. Begin on scrapbook..

October 17th ...63 degrees, clear. Cool night Slept very well...

October 22nd...Dr. Whitfield calls – get new prescription.

October 23rd ...To office noon – To LH with L and the papers

October 24th Feel poorly. Nothing agrees with in way of food – To PC in PM – about 7 Pm Nettie and Pete drove up – come to take Mr. Carlisle home with them...

October 25th ...Nettie – Pete and Mr. Carlisle getting ready to go Live Oak in the morning.

October 26th ...slept fairly well. A cold night – Folks leave at 8 this AM...Squalls this morning – Must write – Nettie wires reached Live Oak 10 PM. Am feeling worse in PM.

October 27th ...Do not sleep well. Dr Whitfield calls this PM...

October 28th ...At office and proof ad copy – Not feeling as well...Dr. Whitfield here this PM.

October 29th 52 degrees, clear, Cool day – used up all day – from 6 AM on something different in my stomach – Dr. Whitfield called – Miss G (possibly Grace) home with L. Ebba here 2 til 5 – Slept last night – but gone to pieces when I got up – at home all day.

At 10:20 on the evening of October 29th, George passed away at his home. One of the tributes published in his obituary was this:

"He may well be called the Father of Panama City, for it was through his vision that the groundwork was laid, the first railroad brought to our shores, with all of its attendant developments."

Lillian West continued to run the publishing company with as many as 16 employees into the 1930's and continued to leave her influence on the area. She sold the St. Andrews Bay News to the Panama City Herald in 1937. It became today's News Herald. She continued commercial printing for many years. Her tax return in 1939 reflected her income that year was $3,328.00, or $64 a week.

She constructed the log cabin on the West property in the 1930's and moved out of the original West home. Mary E. Jones, known as Aunt Mary to the descendants, and Lillian became very close. Mary was possibly a cousin of Lillian's. In 1936 Lillian penned a hand written Last Will on Publishing Company letterhead, and in it bequeathed most of her holdings to Mary. That was later changed.

On April 8th, 1942, Edward H. De Groot, Jr., an attorney in Washington, D.C., and an investor in the Gulf Coast Development Company wrote

Mary Jones (L) and Lillian West at Christmas time in the log cabin Lillian built in the 1930's. BCPL

Lillian. It had been announced that 33 Liberty cargo vessels would be built at Panama City's Wainwright Shipyard. George West's dream of a significant port in Panama City was finally realized, but unfortunately he did not live to see it, wrote De Groot.

Lillian responded patriotically to the call for citizens to support the war effort when America entered World War II. In 1944 at the announcement of a round of War Bonds being offered Lillian wrote to all the stockholders of the Gulf Coast Development Company. One such letter was to Blanch Simmons, a sister of Luella, George's 2nd wife. Lillian said she thought of Blanch often since the death of Luella in 1908, and since George's death in 1926. Her letter to one stockholder,

Mrs. Seniff, said "My heart goes out to you in the burden that you are forced to bear at this time (Mrs. Seniff had at least 2 sons in the war). If George (George Francis West) can shoot Germans as well as he could cats when he visited us several years ago, he ought to be able to halt them." St. Andrews had once been infested with strays that killed chickens and carried rabies, and on a visit there George had apparently rid the community of several diseased cats.

Her message to Gulf Coast Development Company stockholders was clear: "… I was fortunate in negotiating a deal which enables me to place in the Commercial Bank of Panama City…one ($100.00) hundred dollar War Bond for your name ….in exchange of your Gulf Coast Development Company stock certificate. You will please return this certificate to the bank ….at your earliest convenience." She did not leave the exchange open for discussion, and used the exchange to close out the Gulf Coast Development Company forever.

George's great-great grandson Charles Alderman West, Jr. continued to operate the Panama City Publishing Company from 1966 until 2005 when the City of Panama City purchased the building for a museum and historical showplace for the community.

Charles Alderman "Buddy" West, 2009, GMW Collection

Final Days of West Family Members

Margaret Betti "Maggie" Alderman West died in 1931 and is buried in the West family plot at Oakland Cemetery, Panama City, Florida.

Philip Brown West, Sr.

Philip B. West Sr. died at 47 from a sudden heart attack in 1935 while traveling on a train just north of Columbia, S. C. He was buried in Oakland Cemetery in an unmarked grave next to his wife Maggie. He was born in Escanaba, Delta Co., MI where both his parents and grandparents lived at that time. He was raised by his grandfather George M. West after the early death of his parents. He received his education in the schools of Escanaba, MI then attended high school at Oak Park, Chicago Heights, Illinois and then attended Wabash College in Indiana, where he was a member of Phi Delta Theta fraternity.

George Francis West,
Courtesy Buddy West,
BCPL

George Francis West, the eldest great grandson of George West, served in the Navy in World War II. On April 8th, 1940 he wrote to his Grandmama, Lillian, and asked her to help him get to Brooklyn, New York so he could re-enlist in the Navy. He needed money to get to New York. He was living in Lenoir, North Carolina, as were Charles, Pert (Sara), and Phil. He reported them all to be well, but unable to help him financially. He did re-enlist but the ship he was assigned to was lost off Trinidad in 1942 with no survivors. He was 32 years old.

His last letter to Lillian was as follows:

May ___, 1942 (date removed by the Navy)

Port of Spain, Trinidad

Dear Grandmama,

Will be back in States in a couple of mo. Intend to come down to Fla. for a few days to see you. Have been doing ok just knocking around from here to there. Give everyone my best.

Love, George

Years later in 1953 Lillian West wrote to George and the letter was returned to her.

October 10th, 1953

Dearest George,

Your last letter to me dated May ___, 1942 has always been in my top drawer of desk, since I received it – and I read and re-read it over and over again – Some how, I still look for you to come home as promised in this letter - Although the government has reported to Grace that you went down on some boat. Somehow I have always felt that you were in some foreign port – or maybe back on some island with one of the girls you use to play around with – If you get this letter please write me a note.

Lots of Love,

Grandmama

Marion Rawls "Bay" and Lucille West, Courtesy Buddy West, BCPL

Marion Rawls West, known as "Bay", was third great grandson of George West. He married Lucille Jones and lived in Philadelphia where he was attending school at Temple University. On a visit to Florida in 1947, the couple was tragically killed in a car crash at Hwy 231(State Rd 75) and Hwy 20. The car was traveling too fast when making the turn onto State Rd 75. Bay was 34 years old. The driver of the car was charged with manslaughter.

Grace's second husband, John Stephen Wilson died in 1956 and was entombed at Greenwood Cemetery, Panama City, Florida.

Grace and A. B.'s daughter Eleanor Rose Joyner Furman died in 1963 and is buried in the West family plot at Oakland Cemetery adjacent to her father.

Philip Brown West, Jr., the fourth and youngest great grandson of George M. West was living in North Carolina and on Christmas Eve 1964 fatally shot himself at home. His wife, Elizabeth Beach West, and children were home at the time.

Lillian Carlisle West, c. 1932, GMW Collection, BCPL

Lillian Carlisle West died August 26th, 1970 and was interred at the Millville Cemetery in Panama City, Florida.

Grace West Wilson,
Courtesy Wilson
Funeral Home

Grace West Wilson died in 1980 and is entombed at Greenwood Cemetery in Panama City, Florida.

Charles Alderman West, Sr.,
Courtesy Buddy West, BCPL

Charles Alderman West, Sr., second born great-grandson of George M. West, married Sara Gertrude Councill on February 24th, 1935 at St. James Episcopal Church in Lenoir, North Carolina. She was dressed in a mid-calf navy dress, hat, and gloves. They borrowed a car and went to Asheville, North Carolina for their wedding night. They moved to Panama City in 1958 and Charles operated the Panama City Publishing Company until about 1975. He passed away in 1981 in Panama City, Florida. Sara passed away in 2011.

Betty Jean Wilson Normand, daughter of Grace (West) Wilson and John Stephen Wilson died in 1999 and was interred at Greenwood Cemetery, Panama City, Florida, adjacent to her parents.

APPENDIX

ONLINE RESOURCES FOR ADDITIONAL READING:

www.nwrls.com   Bay County Public Library

https://archive.org/details/williamwestofsci00west

"William West of Scituate, Rhode Island" is also available through the Bay County Public Library Local History Room

"Cruise of the Jane Anderson" is available through the Bay County Public Library Local History Room

www.brandonlibrary.net/brandontimes

www.deltahistorical.org   Delta County Historical Society, Escanaba, Michigan

www.flhiddentreasures.com   Panama City Pilot and St. Andrews Bay News

West Lineage

1   Francis West – came from Salisbury, England sometime before 1639

⬇

2   Peter b. 1637

⬇

3   William b. 1683

⬇

4   William Jr – Lt Gov and Judge, RI b. 1733

⬇

5   John b. 1752

⬇

6   Freeman 1773-1848

⬇

7   Philander Bailey 1814-1886   1841 m. Fidelia Mason 1816-1875

⬇

Children of Philander and Fidelia:
8 Charles Arthur 1842-1862   George Mortimer 1845-1926   Twins: Ellen 1849-1862 & Helen 1849-1859

⬇

Children of George & Adella Melvina Showers West m. 1865:   1909 m. Lillian Carlisle:
9   Charles Ernest 1866-1892   unnamed infant daughter   twins that died at birth (w/Lillian)

⬇

Children of Charles Ernest and Eleanor "Nellie" Brown West:
10 Philip Brown Sr. 1888-1935   Ernest Warren (twin b/d 1888)   Grace Hughwitt 1890-1980
   1909 m. Margaret Betti Alderman   1912 m. Alpheus Baker Joyner
                                                       1923 m. John Stephen Wilson

⬇

                                            Daughter of Alpheus and Grace:
                                            Eleanor Rose Joyner (Furman) 1915-1963

                                         Daughter of Stephen and Grace:
                                         Betty Jean Wilson (Normand) 1923-1999

Children of Philip and Maggie:
11 George Francis 1910-1942   Charles Alderman 1911-1981   Marion Rawls "Bay" 1914-1947   Philip Jr 1916-1964

⬇   ⬇

                                                           m. Elizabeth Beach
Children of Charles and Sara Gertrude (Councill) West: Children of Phil Jr & Elizabeth:
12   Betti   Charles Alderman Jr   Margaret   Ann Barbette, Susan, Libby

Ancestry of George Mortimer West

The First Generation of Wests in America

Francis West arrived in Duxbury, Massachusetts from Salisbury, England, sometime prior to 1639, and for years to come West descendants would disperse in New England, the mid-west, and Florida. Francis married Margaret Reeves on February 27th, 1639 and they had five children: Samuel, Thomas, Peter, Mary, and Ruth. He was listed as a surveyor of highways in Duxbury and was also a house carpenter. The Plymouth colony records show that he made a pair of stocks for the town of Duxbury in 1640. He was admitted "freeman" in Plymouth Colony in 1656, meaning he was a citizen of the Colony, possessed the right to vote for Governor and Assistants, and the right to hold office. This has often been viewed by historians as one of the earliest forms of demand for representative government and individual rights in America. However, women and servants were not eligible for freeman status. He served as Constable in 1661, and was a member of the "Grand Enquest" in 1662, '69, '74, '78, '80, and '81. Serving as a member of the Grand Enquest, he and other appointed members would hear suspected criminal charges against members in the Colony, and if found credible, the guilty would be tried in the appropriate court. This special jury of freemen would also hold accountable the political leaders of the day. The jury could require officers of the Colony, freemen, deputies, and town officials to appear before the jury for failure to uphold duties, take the required oaths, attend sessions, maintain the prisons or highways entrusted to their care by the General Court and laws of the Colony. Usually a fine was the punishment for one found guilty. To serve in these appointed positions Francis West must have been of good character and an

242

honorable citizen in Duxbury. Francis remained in Duxbury his entire life, to age 86, passing away on January 2, 1692.

The Second Generation

Francis' third son, Peter, was born around 1647-48. He resided in Duxbury, and married a woman named Patience. Between 1675 and 1697 they had 9 children: Mary (who died young), Margaret, Esther, Ann, William, Mary, Benjamin, Elisha, and Samuel. There may have been other children as William is sometimes referenced as the 6th child. Little is known about Peter.

The Third Generation

The 1st son (5th child) of Peter and Patience, William, was born May 4th. The family moved to North Kingston, Rhode Island. However, historically there has been considerable debate about whether Peter, or if there was another son of Francis', also named Francis, was the father of William. A New England Historian, Dr. Edward E. Cornwall and genealogist Miss Guild of Providence, Rhode Island offer differing views on the descent. The difference appears to be that Miss Guild declares Francis had a son named Francis, but Cornwall, and the family records have no such entry. George M. West chose to follow Dr. Cornwall and the family records.

The Fourth Generation

William married Abiah Sprague in 1709 and they had a son, William Jr., born in North Kingston, R. I. It was said William West Jr. lived 83 years and died around 1816, putting his birth about 1733. There is very little documented information about any other children, and even the birth date of William Jr. is unknown.

The census of 1774 documents that William Jr. was married to Eleanor Brown, and had 6 sons and 6 daughters in the home. The known children were: William, Charles, John (born around 1752), Samuel, Hiram, Elsie, Olive, Ellen, Sally, and Hannah. A daughter named Almy or Amy, and a son named Thomas may also have been there. William Jr. and Eleanor moved from North Kingston to Scituate, Rhode Island around 1758. William West, Jr., also known as General West or William West of Scituate, became a Judge and Lt. Governor in Rhode Island, and his life, like so many early settlers, was wrought with both joy and tragedy. He was gifted as an innkeeper, farmer, in real estate, and as Colonel and Brigadier General in the Colonial Army during the Revolutionary War. He failed as a privateer though, losing 2 ships and cargo. His public service to the Colony came with no financial compensation and he died destitute, living with his son Samuel. His story is documented in a book, *William West, Jr. of Scituate, R.I.*, written and published by George M. West in 1919. With that book being available digitally through the Bay County Public Library, Local History Room, this portion about William Jr. is abbreviated in order to devote more text to the remainder of West descendants.

William West house, built 1775,

From cemetery across the road from the house
Courtesy Margaret West Matheson, BCPL

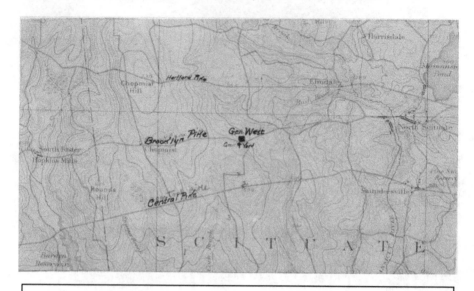

Location of William West house and cemetery, Courtesy Margaret West Matheson, BCPL

The Fifth Generation

John West, lived in a house near his parents, William Jr. and Eleanor. John West and his first wife, had 2 children, a daughter and a son. Their son Freeman was born May 27th, 1773. Though there is a different date shown for Freeman's birth in one place in the genealogy, this one is consistently used in other places.

In the 1774 census John is documented as the head of his home in Scituate, with no females over 16, indicating he was a widower. The census does list a boy and a girl under the age of 16, making 3 in the family, a father and 2 children. John West was raising 2 very young children on his own. He enlisted in November, 1776 in the Rhode Island Militia for a year, then again in 1778 and was in the Battle of Rhode Island in July 1778. The census of 1790 reveals John remarried and lists that his home held 12 people, including a male over sixteen, a wife, and 9 females. Little else is known about John, other than he lived 83 years.

The Sixth Generation

Freeman West married Sally Salsbury and they eventually settled in Sangerfield, Oneida County, New York where Freeman was a farmer. He and Sally had 4 children: Joshua, born April 8th, 1801, Joseph, born January 29th, 1805, Marcelia, born May 14th, 1808, and Philander Bailey West, born December 24th, 1814. Freeman lived 75 years, passing away December 14th, 1848.

The Seventh Generation

Philander Bailey West lived from 1814 to 1886. He married Fidelia Mason in 1841, and she lived from 1816 to 1875. Their children were Charles Arthur West, George Mortimer West, and twins Helen M. and Ellen M. West.

Written by George West about himself in 1926

Data George Mortimer West Biography.

First appearance in Public Directory was in "Poor's Directory of Railway officials", published in 1887. That was the second annual number of the first publication of Railway Officials. Have never seen the First Annual. In this directory on page 151, Officials of the C. & N. W. R. R. is to be found the following: Peninsula Division- 425 miles. W. B. Linsley, Superintendent; George M. West, Assistant Superintendent; J. Symons, Master Mechanic.

From "Biographical Directory ofRailway Officials of America," 1906 issue, the following is taken: "West, George M., General Superintendent Chicago Heights Terminal Transfer Rd. Office Chicago Heights, Illm. Born Nov. 28th, 1845. Entered railway service 1859, since which he has been consecutively to 1861, helper in warehouse and clerk , Milwaukee & Horicon 1861 to 1869,
Ry.; operator and agent Chicago, Milwaukee& St Paul Ry., 1869 to 1872 publishing newspapers and practising law; 1872 , operator Chicago & Northwestern Ry at Ishpemeing , Mich. ,; August 1872 to 1886 train dispatcher and chief train dispatcher at Escanaba; 1886 to 1900 assistant superintendent Peninsula division same road at Escanaba, Mich.;; 1900 to 1902 , superintendent Chicago Heights Terminal Transfer Rd.; 1902 to date,(1906) general superintendent same road.

The "Who's Who in Finance and Banking" issue of 1922 we take the following: West George Mortimer, Panama City, Fla. Publisher, editor, promoter; born Oneida county, N. Y., Nov 28th, 1845; son Philander B. and Fidelia)Mason) West; educated in common schools New York and Wisconsin; married, first, Adella M. Showers(d); second Luella V. Simmons(d);,third, Lillian Carlisle ; one son ; Charles E. by first wife. Began railway work at age of fifteen; was with Milwaukee & Horicon Railroad and its successor, Chicago, Milwaukee & St Paul Railroad, 1860 to 1870; also established and published Brandon,(Wis) Times; published Ripon Free-Press 1870-72, admitted

to bar 18 71; . Entered service of Chicago & Northwestern Railroad, 1872;
Upper Michigan, train dispatcher; became assistant superintendent until
1900, then took superintendcy of Chicago Heights Terminal Transfer Railroad
Chicago Heights, Ill ; remined as superintendent and general superintendent
until 1906; removed to Panama City, Fla., purchased old town sibes and
founded town of Panama City; secured railroad connection andpromoted the
building of the town. Vice-president and General Managerof Gulf Coast Development Company, owners of town site; active in securing appropriation for
improvement of St Andrews Bay harbor, 1909-10, and also first link in
interzoastal canal; foubder and editor of Panama Cit y Pilot since 1906,
and St Andrews Bay News since 1916. Has written various articles and papers
on wild flowers of great north woods, camping in Florida, genealogy of
General West, Rhode Island; railway management; State control of railways;
History of St Andrews. Member Sons of American Revolution; Old Time Tele-
graphers' Association. Recreation : A study of the Flora , Fauna and Ceolay
of West Florida . Independent in politics. Methodist."

1922 to 1926.

Data. The Lady Elgin was sunk on the morning of Sept 8th, 1860. I was
acting operator at Waupun, Wis., at that time.

The Milwaukee & Horicon R. R. was finished to Brandon, Wis., Oct
15th, 1856. When mother and us children came to Brandon, the rails were
just laid to the station. Grading was being done 500 feet north of
the station.

George West Reading List

Lorna Doone, 1869, by Richard Doddridge Blackmore, a romance based on a group of historical characters and set in the late 17th century England. Blackmore was one of the most famous English novelists of the second half of the nineteenth century, acclaimed for vivid descriptions and personification of the countryside.

The Colonel's Daughter, 1883, an early novel of a soldier's story by Charles King.

A War Time Wooing, 1888, a Civil War tale by Charles King, who would also later write scripts for Buffalo Bill Cody's silent films.

Haydn's Dictionary of Dates, 1866, by Benjamin Vincent. A universal reference relating to all ages and nations.

The Led-Horse Claim, 1883, a romance of a mining camp, by Mary Hallock Foote, an American author and illustrator best known for her illustrated short stories and novels portraying life in the mining communities of the turn-of-the-century American West.

Jane Eyre, 1847, by Charlotte Bronte

A Daughter of Heth, 1871, a romance novel by William Black

Hermann & Dorothea, an epic poem, an idyll, by German writer Johann Wolfgang von Goethe between 1796 and 1797. Set around 1792 at the beginning of the French Revolutionary Wars, when French forces under General Custine invaded and briefly occupied parts of the Palatinate.

Wake Robin, 1871, the first of over thirty books written by John Burroughs. Regarded as the father of the American nature essay, Burroughs was one of the most popular authors of his time. His writing journey began while a clerk in Washington DC during the Civil War, recounting tales of birds and his ramblings in his native Catskills.

Bryant's History of the US, 1876, by William Cullen Bryant and Sydney Howard Gay who eventually wrote 23 more volumes of history.

The Gold Bug, 1843, by Edgar Allen Poe

The Cloven Foot, 1879, by Mary Elizabeth Braddon, English author of Victorian "sensation" novels. An extremely prolific writer, she produced some 75 novels with very inventive plots.

Daisy Thornton, 1878, by Mary Jane Holmes, a bestselling and prolific American author who wrote 39 popular novels, as well as short stories. Her first novel sold 250,000 copies; and she had total sales of 2 million books in her lifetime, second only to Harriet Beecher Stowe. Portraying domestic life in small town and rural settings, she examined gender relationships, as well as those of class and race. She also dealt with slavery and the American Civil War, with a strong sense of moral justice. Her popular work was excluded from most 19th-century literary histories, but she has received recognition and reappraisal since the late 20th century.

Far From the Madding Crowd, by Thomas Hardy

A Modern Instance, a realistic novel written by William Dean Howells, and published in 1882. The novel is about the deterioration of a once loving marriage under the influence of capitalistic greed. It is the first American novel by a canonical author to seriously consider divorce as a realistic outcome of marriage. George commented about the book: "A goodly amount of human nature as it really is – to be found in it".

Poem of Philander Bailey West

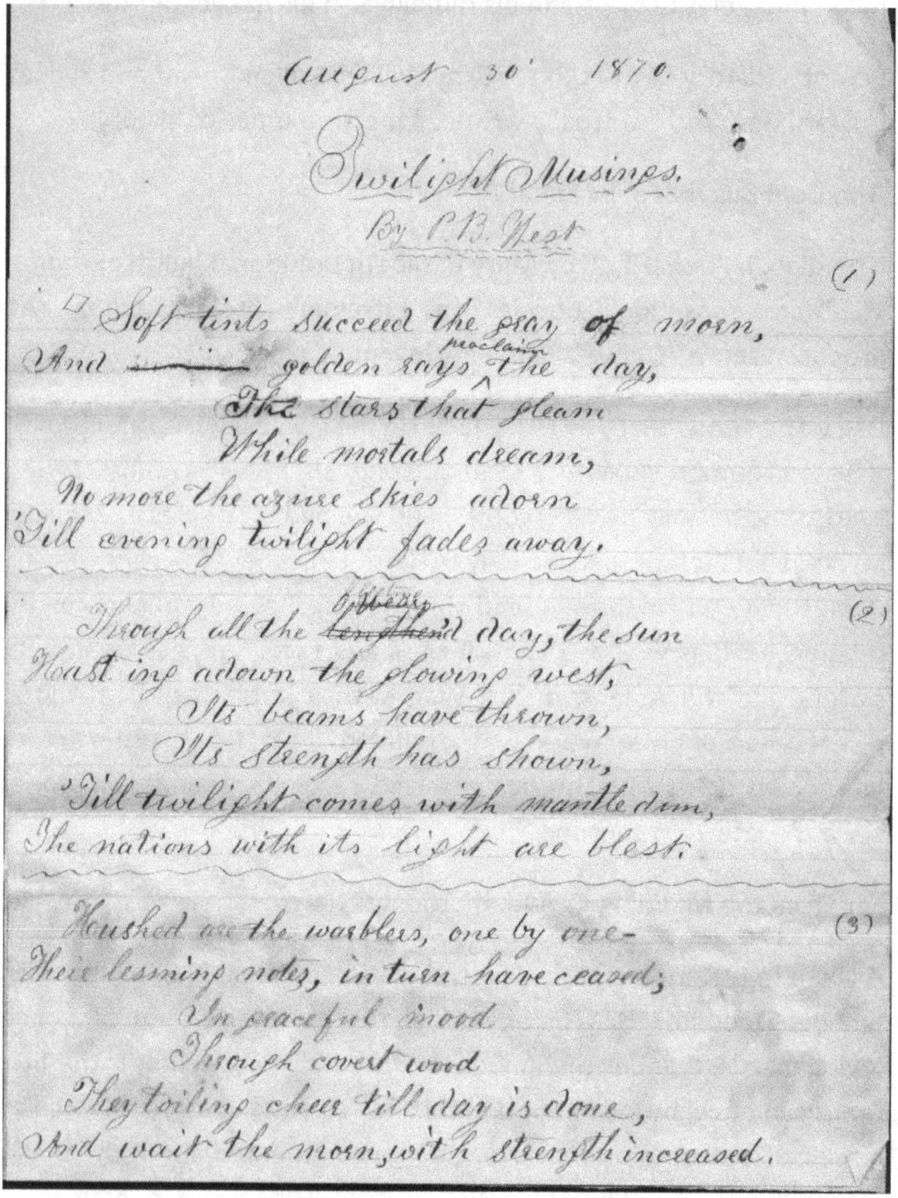

August 30' 1870.

Twilight Musings.

By P. B. West

(1)

Soft tints succeed the gray of morn,
And ——— proclaim golden rays the day,
The stars that gleam
While mortals dream,
No more the azure skies adorn
'Till evening twilight fades away.

(2)

Through all the ^weary day, the sun
Hasting adown the glowing west,
Its beams have thrown,
Its strength has shown,
'Till twilight comes with mantle dim,
The nations with its light are blest.

(3)

Hushed are the warblers, one by one—
Their lessening notes, in turn have ceased;
In peaceful mood
Through covert wood
They toiling cheer till day is done,
And wait the morn, with strength increased.

Then rest ye weary- sweet the hour -
Night's shadows o'er the landscape creep;
Then in love's urn,
Fresh incense burn;
As dew in the closing flower,
The pure in heart- as softly sleep.

Life's morning blushes as the dawn,
Life's noon-day strength, like potent ray
Of ruling sun.
As shadows dun
If hope and love are e'er withdrawn,
The close of life's eventful day.

In darkness beams of hope arise,
Life's twilight comes not unforeseen;
As dew in flowers
In sunlit hours,
Hope brightest shines—in sweet surprise,
Reflecting holy light - serene.

Employment Application Supplementary by Philip B. West, Sr.

over ⟶

Lenoir, North Carolina,
June 28, 1933.

Personnel Officer,
Tennessee Valley Authority,
Washington, D. C.

Dear Sir:

In presenting my application for employment, I wish to submit the following supplementary data:

Education: I was unable to attend school regularly owing to frequent changes of residence in search of a climate that would benefit the health of my grandmother, my grandparents having taken me to rear following the death of my parents. This lack was offset by studies under several competent tutors at home. I was forced to leave college in 1907 when my grandfather suffered financial reverses. Under my step-grandmother, nee Louella Y. Simmons, for some years a member of the faculty of Chicago University, I pursued an extended course of home study and selected reading. These advantages, taken with years of newspaper work, have given me a fund of useful knowledge superior to that possessed by the average college graduate.

Specialized Work: From 1913 to 1925 I was deputy clerk of the Circuit Court in Bay County, Fla., in charge of map filings and highway data for the county. In this position I built up a considerable practice as title examiner. From June, 1925, to January, 1927, I had charge of the office of the Panama Abstract & Title Co., of which I was one of the principal owners. My duties included supervision of photostatic take-off, assembling and checking of abstracts of title. I have done map drafting ever since leaving college.

Employment and Idle Periods: My employment with the Panama City Publishing Company, 1909 to 1921, was under direction of my grandfather, the late Geo. M. West, owner and editor of The Panama City Pilot, who passed away in October, 1926, in consequence of which I can not give him as a reference. Mr. Meates, named in the application, was associated with me while with the publishing company. Following my retirement as manager of the Panama Abstract & Title Co., in January, 1927, I suffered a physical breakdown from which I have only recently recovered. I am now able to put in a full day's work six days a week. The mild diabetes from which I suffer does not hamper me in any way.

I am without regular employment yielding sufficient return to provide me with the necessities of life and have the greatest need of work. I am willing to go anywhere I may be sent and do any work within the scope of my experience and training.

Respectfully,

Philip B. West

INDEX

CPSIA information can be obtained
at www.ICGtesting.com
Printed in the USA
FSHW021559260221
78945FS